USN F-4 PHANTOM II
VS
VPAF MiG-17/19

Vietnam War 1965–73

PETER DAVIES

First published in Great Britain in 2009 by Osprey Publishing,
Midland House, West Way, Botley, Oxford OX2 0PH, UK
443 Park Avenue South, New York, NY 10016, USA
E-mail: info@ospreypublishing.com

A CIP catalogue record for this book is available from the British Library

Print ISBN 978 1 84603 475 6
PDF e-book ISBN 978 1 84908 134 4

Edited by Tony Holmes
Cover artwork and battlescene by Gareth Hector
Cockpit, gunsight artwork by Jim Laurier
Three-views and armament scrap views by Jim Laurier
Page layout by Ken Vail Graphic Design, Cambridge, UK
Index by Alan Thatcher
Typeset in ITC Conduit and Adobe Garamond
Maps by Bounford.com, Cambridge, UK
Originated by PDQ Digital Media Solutions, Suffolk, UK
Printed in China through Bookbuilders

09 10 11 12 13   10 9 8 7 6 5 4 3 2 1

Osprey Publishing is supporting the Woodland Trust, the UK's leading
woodland conservation charity, by funding the dedication of trees.

FOR A CATALOGUE OF ALL BOOKS PUBLISHED BY OSPREY
MILITARY AND AVIATION PLEASE CONTACT:

Osprey Direct, c/o Random House Distribution Center,
400 Hahn Road, Westminster, MD 21157
Email: uscustomerservice@ospreypublishing.com

Osprey Direct, The Book Service Ltd, Distribution Centre,
Colchester Road, Frating Green, Colchester, Essex, CO7 7DW
E-mail: customerservice@ospreypublishing.com

www.ospreypublishing.com

F-4J Phantom II cover art

May 10, 1972 was the US Navy's most successful day against the Vietnamese
People's Air Force (VPAF). Amongst the Naval Aviators to enjoy success on
this date were Lts Matt Connelly and Tom Blonski in F-4J BuNo 155769 of
top-scoring squadron VF-96 from USS *Constellation* (CVA-64). Tasked with
flying a TARCAP (Target Area Combat Air Patrol) for a Hai Duong
marshalling yard strike, Connelly and Blonksi, in "Showtime 106", and their
wingman Lt Aaron Campbell saw two MiG-17Fs from the 923rd Fighter
Regiment (FR) pursuing an A-7A Corsair II. Diving after the enemy fighter,
Blonski set his radar up to fire an AIM-7E medium range air-to-air missile.
This weapon system failed, however, so Connelly switched to the short range
AIM-9G Sidewinder instead. Having unsuccessfully fired at one MiG, he
spotted four more VPAF fighters off to his right. Connelly slowed and shot
another AIM-9G at one that had fatally rolled "wings level". His "snap shot"
at high overtake scorched his own jet's extended speed brakes, but destroyed
the MiG nevertheless. Seconds later Connolly saw another MiG-17 to his
right whose pilot had made the same mistake of rolling 'wings level', thus
providing the F-4 pilot with a stable Sidewinder target. The missile's
expanding rod warhead severed the MiG's tail. Heading out, Connelly fired
at a third MiG-17 and distracted a fourth jet from shooting at squadronmate
Lt Randy Cunningham's F-4J by firing a ballistic AIM-7 close to it.
(Artwork by Gareth Hector from an F-4 model by Thierry Nyssen)

MiG-17F cover art

Snr Lts Le Hai and Nguyen Dinh Phuc, with Ho Van Quy and Nguyen Phi
Hung (all from the 923rd FR), intercepted a TARCAP of F-4B Phantom IIs
from VF-151, embarked in USS *Coral Sea* (CVA-43), as they followed A-4E
Skyhawks out after a Haiphong strike on November 19, 1967. The MiGs,
deployed to a forward airfield at Kien An, attacked F-4B BuNo 150997, call
sign "Switchbox 110", flown by Lt Cdr Doug Clower and Lt(jg) Walt Estes,
who retaliated with two Sidewinders just before their right wing was blown
off. Lt Cdr Clower was the only survivor. He assured the author that his
aircraft was hit by an "Atoll" from a MiG-21, and two of these fighters were
seen operating with the MiG-17s that day. His wingman in "Switchbox 115"
was Lt(jg) Jim Teague, with RIO Lt(jg) Ted Stier. Their aircraft was
surrounded by tracers from the MiG-17s, and probably ingested debris from
Clower's exploding Phantom II. "Switchbox 115" entered a flat spin, from
which only Stier was able to escape, joining Clower in captivity. Both Clower
and Estes were awarded an unofficial MiG kill, while Le Hai claimed
Clower's F-4B as his fourth victory. Nguyen Dinh Phuc claimed the other
Phantom II. "Switchbox 110" was one of the F-4Bs originally loaned to the
USAF as F-110As. "Red 3020" was Le Hai's assigned MiG-17F, and it was
also flown by Ngo Duc Dao and Nguyen Van Bay the Younger, who was
killed in the aircraft on May 6, 1972 probably in combat with the VF-51
F-4B crewed by Lt Cdr Jerry Houston and Lt Kevin Moore. (Artwork by
Gareth Hector from a MiG-17 model by Wiek Luijken)

Acknowledgements

I am grateful to the following for their assistance with this book – Capt
George Baldry, USN (Ret.), Lt Henry A. Bartholomay, USN (Ret.), Lt
David Batson, USN (Ret.), Lt Lynn Batterman, USN (Ret.), Capt "Hap"
Chandler, USN (Ret.), Cdr C. Douglas Clower, USN (Ret.), Cdr David
Daniels, USN (Ret.), Cdr Curtis Dosé, USN (Ret.), Capt Orville Elliott,
USN (Ret.), Cdr William Freckleton, USNR (Ret.), Capt Brian Grant, USN
(Ret.), Capt Jerry B. Houston, USN (Ret.), Lt Fritz Klumpp, USN
(Ret)/McDonnell Douglas, Capt Eugene P. Lund, USN (Ret.), Attila Mates,
Cdr Peter B. Mersky, USNR (Ret.), Capt John Nash, USN (Ret.), Grp Capt
Mike Shaw, RAF (Ret.), Mrs Susan Teague, Dr István Toperczer and Col
Ralph Wetterhahn, USAF (Ret.).

CONTENTS

INTRODUCTION

Although the Vietnam War appeared to most impartial observers as a conflict in which the world's major superpower failed to suppress a poorly-equipped guerrilla army, the air war brought the most advanced defence technologies of both the USA and the USSR into direct conflict. It also served as a laboratory for many of the technical advances that have sustained the world's defence equipment manufacturers since then.

For the US Navy, it was the first opportunity to combat-test its supersonic missile-armed F-4 Phantom II fighter. Also, the British-designed angled deck had revolutionised carrier operations and made large-scale "Alpha" strikes possible. However, the US Navy also learned that the recently discarded art of air-to-air dogfighting could not be replaced so easily, and as MiG killer John Nichols pointed out, "We Americans have a tendency to trust technology more than skill, but we periodically rediscover the truth".

Nichols was an F-8 Crusader pilot, and Naval Aviators flying this aircraft had been the last to be trained in air-to-air gunnery. Indeed, the US Navy's Fleet Air Gunner Unit (FAGU) had been closed in 1960, and F-8 "gunfighters" were the custodians of skills that were assumed to be redundant in a missile age. Their elite ethos lived on too. MiG killer Jerry B. Houston recalled that "only the top ten per cent of pilot graduates were even considered for the F-8 pipeline. They ate, breathed, thought and dreamed about fighting enemy aeroplanes all the time".

The first newly trained F-4B pilots had different ambitions based on their aircraft's intended role as a long-range interceptor that relied on state-of-the-art missiles and radar to prevent advanced Soviet bombers from attacking capital ships. Air-to-air combat at close range hardly featured in the training syllabus, and it was assumed that medium range air-to-air missiles like the AIM-7 Sparrow meant that F-4 crews would rarely see their foe, as their missiles would be launched under radar control, until it became visible as a distant flaming wreck.

Early in the Vietnam War gunfighting and Sidewinder-shooting F-8s certainly did engage MiG-17s, scoring three kills in June 1966. However, the first three MiG kills in 1965 were by F-4Bs using Sparrows.

For MiG-17 pilots of the Vietnamese Peoples' Air Force (VPAF), there was virtually no background of military aviation to draw on. Helped from the outset by the USSR and China, the VPAF traced its origins to 1945, when the fathers of many F-4 crews in Task Force 77 were beating the Imperial Japanese Navy in the Pacific. Two ancient training aircraft were used to lay the foundations for Ho Chi Minh's air force in 1949, while a single Royal Laotian Air Force T-28 that was acquired via a defector in 1963 claimed the VPAF's first air-to-air victory when it shot down an American C-123 on a covert supply mission in February 1964.

Although the French air force was initially the model for the VPAF, its first 110 students went to China for training in 1956, and 30 more were sent to the USSR in 1957 for their first jet experience with the MiG-15. Training in North Vietnam began at Cat Bi, near Haiphong, in 1956, and in 1957 a MiG-17 training unit was set up at Mong Tu, in China, close to the border with Vietnam, using 36 aircraft. These

An F-4J Phantom II of VF-21 about to take the wire on USS *Ranger* (CVA-61) during the squadron's sixth combat cruise in 1970. Having scored the first two official Phantom II MiG kills of the war (on June 17, 1965), VF-21 did not add to its score during its six subsequent cruises. The unit did, however, lose three aircraft to AAA and six to operational accidents. "Sundown 106" is carrying a pair of AIM-9G missiles on its wing pylons, an AIM-7E Sparrow in its forward right missile well and three tanks. A single centreline tank was a more typical fit for F-4s flying from *Yankee Station*. (US Navy via R. L. Lawson)

pilots were the first to enter combat in 1964, and their Chinese base served as a refuge throughout the Vietnam War.

Whereas the major aerial conflicts in earlier wars had usually matched opposing fighter types fairly evenly, the skies over North Vietnam were riven by less obvious opponents. While the US Navy's F-8 Crusader equated to the VPAF's MiG-21 "Fishbed", the two met infrequently in combat. Far more of the duels were between the MiG-17F "Fresco", a simple day fighter which had been conceived in the late 1940s, and America's most complex, costly all-weather interceptor, the mighty F-4 Phantom II.

While the VPAF pilots of the 921st FR "Sao Do", fresh from Mong Tu in 1964, had only just finished their training on the MiG-17, their US Navy counterparts manning fleet F-4B Phantom II units had three years of frontline experience with their new fighter to draw on. However, little of it concerned the kind of fighter-on-fighter combat that the MiG "drivers" had learned from the Korean War experience of their veteran Chinese and Russian instructors.

Eight Atlantic Fleet and eight Pacific Fleet squadrons had F-4Bs and were categorised as deployable by July 1964. Prior to them entering the war zone in Southeast Asia, most of their carrier-borne flying had consisted of intercepting Soviet reconnaissance aircraft that were feeling out the US Navy's fleets' defences during carrier deployments around the globe.

These Cold War missions suited the F-4B concept well. The fighter would catapult-launch, day or night in most weather conditions, with a full missile load, climb at maximum speed to altitude under the guidance of the carrier's radar and then detect targets using its radar for a head-on deterrent interception, usually

One of the best surviving images of VPAF MiGs, this line-up of Noi Bai MiG-21PFMs and MiG-21F-13s in 1972 shows how the MiG-17 (here with ORO-57 unguided rocket pods rather than the usual PTB-400 drop tanks) was being transferred to the ground-attack role by the latter stages of the war. (NVA via Dr István Toperczer)

culminating in a friendly wave to the Russian aircrew. No hard manoeuvring or close fighting was foreseen. In Vietnam, however, the Phantom IIs' escorting tasks would see the jets protecting large air-strike packages, or performing as bombers themselves. When flying these vitally important missions, Naval Aviators quickly discovered that the F-4 was often at a significant tactical disadvantage when engaged by VPAF MiG fighters.

For the MiG-17 pilot, his sole intention was to lure the F-4 crew in their heavy jet into a close dogfight, where the Phantom II's missiles would be useless and the MiG's heavy calibre cannon had free range to inflict mortal damage on American aircraft. There would be no friendly waves from VPAF pilots!

Although many F-8 Crusaders remained in service at the start of the Vietnam War, production had all but ended by 1964 and the US Navy was fully committed to the F-4 as its replacement. It would take at least four years for the Phantom II training syllabus to be modified in order to reinstate the air-to-air skills that Crusader pilots had learned at establishments such as FAGU. Much of that revised doctrine was based on the experience of F-4 pilots during Operation *Rolling Thunder* (which ran from March 3 1965 to October 31 1968), when just nine MiG-17s were shot down by F-4Bs, of which only five were actually claimed by the jet's primary armament, the AIM-7 Sparrow.

A reminder that the US Navy's war was primarily about bombing. All F-4 fighter squadrons would be eligible for flak suppression, strike or less accurate straight-and-level bombing, often on a signal from an A-6 Intruder. In the foreground is the Phantom II flown by Lt "Duke" Cunningham and Lt(jg) "Willie" Driscoll, which became a triple MiG-killer on its final mission on May 10, 1972. (US Navy)

CHRONOLOGY

1945
Summer A Soviet team in Germany discover plans for the swept-wing, jet-powered, Focke-Wulf Ta 183 *Huckebein* fighter.

1948
May McDonnell's FH-1 Phantom becomes the first US jet fighter to operate from an aircraft carrier.

December Using Rolls-Royce Nene turbojets, MiG designers develop the Ta 183 into the MiG-15 and the first production aircraft flies in December 1948.

1950
January 13 SI-2 (MiG-17 prototype) flies for the first time. Production of the fighter begins the following year at five Soviet factories to equip the Warsaw Pact air forces. A total of 10,824 are built, including 1,061 in China as the Shenyang J-5.

1954
February 5 SM-9/1 (MiG-19 prototype) flies, based on the SM-2, a MiG-17 development. The Soviet Air Force duly orders 600 MiG-19s, a small proportion of its target of 16,034 fighters.

1955
June US Navy issues a requirement for a two-seat, long-range fighter interceptor and McDonnell proposes the F3H-G.

1956
March 110 VPAF pilots begin training in China and Russia.

1958
May 8 F3H-G, developed into the F4H-1 Phantom II, makes its first flight.

Autumn Soviet MiG-19 production ends in favour of the MiG-21 and Su-7.

1960
Spring 52 VPAF pilots begin MiG-17 conversion training in China.

December After a series of record-breaking flights the F4H-1 enters service.

1961
September First operational F-4B squadron, VF-74, completes training in September 1961.

1962
May VF-96, with F-4B Phantom IIs, flies patrols from USS *Ranger* (CVA-61) off Vietnam during the Laotian crisis.

December First batches of Soviet and Chinese-trained VPAF MiG-17 pilots return to North Vietnam.

1964
February 3 36 MiG-17 and MiG-15UTI aircraft are donated to the VPAF by the USSR and used to establish the 921st FR "Sao Dao".

May 5 VF-142 and VF-143 begin their first F-4B cruise aboard USS *Constellation* (CVA-64) and make the jet's combat debut over Vietnam in Operation *Pierce Arrow* strikes during August.

August 2 In the Gulf of Tonkin Incident, North Vietnamese P-4 patrol boats attack the destroyer USS *Maddox* (DD-731) as it gathers communications intelligence off North Vietnam. US Navy carriers begin retaliatory air strikes near Vinh.

An F-4B of VF-92 launches at the start of a training mission during *Ranger*'s August 1964–May 1965 Westpac cruise. (via Norman Taylor)

1965

March 15	US Navy flies its first Operation *Rolling Thunder* missions.
April 3	921st FR MiG-17s undertake their first aerial combat when they engage F-8Es of VF-211 without result.
April 9	A VF-96 F-4B becomes the first US Navy Phantom II combat loss, being allegedly downed by MiG-17s from the Chinese Peoples' Liberation Army shortly after its crew had destroyed a communist jet.
June 17	VF-21 score the F-4B's first official VPAF MiG-17 kills.
September 7	Second VPAF MiG-17 unit, the 923rd FR "Yen The", is established at Kep.
October 19	Data-link equipped F-4G Phantom II makes a combat cruise with VF-213.
December	Ten radar-equipped MiG-17PF "Fresco-Ds" arrive from the USSR.

1966

May 27	F-4J Phantom II makes its first flight, entering combat in April 1968.
June 21	MiG-17's first official US Navy kill takes the form of an F-8E from VF-211. By 14 December two F-8Es and eleven USAF aircraft have been lost to MiG-17s according to US records, while VPAF pilots claim 34 kills during the same period.

Four Shenyang J-5s (Chinese-built MiG-17Fs) of the 921st FR are prepared for a mission at Tran Hanh on November 6, 1965. Although the aircraft's wing shared some parts with the flying surface of the earlier MiG-15, it was swept at 45 degrees and more crescent-shaped. (VPAF Museum via Dr István Toperczer)

1967

April–June	Heavy losses to USAF fighters and from airfield attacks badly weaken MiG-17 units.
October 30	Last official F-4B MiG-17 kill of *Rolling Thunder*
November 19	First official F-4B losses to MiG-17s.

1968

September 19	Last F-8 MiG kill. The jet is steadily replaced by the F-4 from now on.

1969

February	925th FR is established, flying the Shenyang J-6 (Chinese-built MiG-19)
March 3	First US Navy *Topgun* class begins at NAS Miramar, California.

1972

April 9	First combat action for the MiG-19S.
April 19	Two MiG-17s bomb the destroyer USS *Higbee* (DD-806).
May 10	Seven MiG-17s are lost to US Navy Phantom IIs. Shenyang J-6/MiG-19s destroy two USAF Phantom IIs.
Summer	Attrition ends MiG-19 operations.
July 11	VF-102 F-4J becomes last US loss to a MiG-17 during the war.
December	For Operation *Linebacker II*, six US Navy carriers are on station with ten F-4 and two F-8 units embarked.

1973

January 12	VF-161 F-4B scores the final aerial victory of the war when it downs a MiG-17. This is the 17th MiG-17 to have been claimed in 1972–73 by a US Navy F-4 for the loss of just one Phantom II (the VF-102 F-4J).

DESIGN AND DEVELOPMENT

F-4B/J PHANTOM II

The success of US naval carrier aviation, notably against Japanese forces during World War II, encouraged naval tacticians to follow the US Army Air Force (USAAF) in exploring the early development of jet aircraft. Two Bell P-59As – the USAAF's first jet fighter – were duly acquired in November 1943 for testing.

Earlier, in January 1942, the Westinghouse Electric Company had received an order for a jet engine, which was designed and built in secret in just 13 months. In December 1942 James S. McDonnell (whose company's only previous original design was the unsuccessful XP-67 long-range twin-propeller fighter project for the USAAF) was asked to build a jet-powered carrier-based fighter. As the first Westinghouse powerplant produced a mere 300lbs of thrust, McDonnell allowed for no fewer than eight engines, each with its own throttle, in his conventional straight-wing proposal.

Soon, 1,600lbs of thrust was achievable from the 19-inch diameter Westinghouse WE-19XB-2B turbojet engine. The dimensions of the latter were dictated by the width of the wing, as it was assumed that the engines (two for the McDonnell fighter) would have to be wing-mounted rather than squeezed into the fuel-containing fuselage. Jets were already known to require far more fuel than the piston-driven models they were designed to replace.

Christened the Phantom, the prototype McDonnell XFD-1 made its first flight – powered by a solitary WE-19XB-2B, as this was all that was available at the time – on January 2, 1945.

The end of the war saw production of the redesignated FH-1 Phantom cut from 100 to 60 aircraft, but the type nevertheless provided valuable jet experience for both the US Navy and the fighter's manufacturer. It also helped to establish McDonnell (along with Douglas, Grumman and Vought) in a "paternal relationship" as a supplier of naval aircraft, reinforced by the initiation of his F2H Banshee programme in February 1945.

Despite aeronautical industry cutbacks in 1946, McDonnell was able to move his company into a large plant in St Louis and set up F2H production, for which the Korean War brought big orders. Basically a scaled-up FH-1 Phantom, the Banshee gave the company experience in adapting a design for a variety of roles, including atomic attack, nightfighting, all-weather fighter and reconnaissance, mainly by revising the aircraft's nose configuration. This enabled McDonnell to embark on longer production runs, and these in turn set the scene for the multi-role F-4 Phantom II.

Two other influential designs followed the F2H. McDonnell had secured a USAF contract in 1953 for its F-101 Voodoo, which was to serve as a Strategic Air Command bomber escort fighter. Subsequent variants performed the nuclear strike mission, undertook tactical reconnaissance and, finally, all-weather interception when modified into a two-seater.

Preceding the F-101 by four years, the XF3H-1 Demon was the next McDonnell naval design to achieve series production. Ordered in prototype form in September 1949 and flown for the first time on August 7, 1951, the Demon subsequently enjoyed mixed fortunes in fleet service. The single-engined F3H, had been conceived as a long-range interceptor to compensate for the shortcomings of the Grumman F11F Tiger and Douglas F4D Skyray. Although ordered in quantity by the US Navy a full five months before its first flight, the F3H-1N proved to be an abject failure because of the poor performance of its Westinghouse J40 engine. Created specifically for the US Navy, this powerplant failed to deliver sufficient thrust for the increasingly heavy F3H design, and this duly meant that none of the 58 -1Ns that were built entered fleet service.

The first F4H-1 BuNo 142259 performs taxi trials in May 1958 with its main landing gear doors removed. It has the original pointed nose (for the 24-inch radar dish of the AN/APQ-50 radar) seen on the first 17 Phantom II aircraft. BuNo 142259 also boasted only a single Stanley ejection seat, as the rear cockpit contained test equipment. Despite the aircraft's marriage of engines and air intakes being one of its best design features, they too were gradually reshaped as development progressed. When the prototype first flew on May 27, 1958, more than 6.8 million man hours had already gone into the project. (McDonnell-Douglas via John Harty)

An order for 140 F3H-2N Demons fitted with Allison J71 engines kept McDonnell in business, and provided experience in developing an interceptor that used both Sparrow radar-guided and Sidewinder infrared missiles. The latter jet was designated the F3H-2M, and 80 were built, followed by 239 F3H-2s multi-role strike fighters. The Demon remained in frontline service with the US Navy until 1964.

Chastened by the F3H-1N debacle, and the general underperformance of the various frontline jet fighters picked for the fleet in the early 1950s, naval planners urgently issued a request for a better all-weather fighter in 1953. In June of the following year, McDonnell, after pressing for more US Navy work, was invited to submit proposals for a two-seat radar carrying aircraft. Its F3H-G/H design subsequently won a $38 million development contract against competition from Grumman and North American. Two prototypes were ordered, although the details of the requirement were still very unclear.

Shortly afterwards the project, re-designated AH-1, moved from the fighter to the attack aircraft branch of naval planning, where it was duly changed to include ten pylons for the attack role, four 20mm cannon and a single-seat cockpit. In December 1954 the project was capriciously returned to the US Navy's fighter department, at which point McDonnell put David S. Lewis and Herman D. Barkey in charge of the aircraft. Under their leadership, work quickly commenced on the redesignated F4H-1 programme (known as Design 98 by the manufacturer).

Beginning with a twin-engined F3H-based concept, McDonnell chose either the British (J65) Sapphire or the new up-and-coming, USAF-sponsored, General Electric J79 as the powerplant for the fighter. The latter was designed to deliver unprecedented thrust for sustained supersonic flight by the B-58 Hustler bomber and F-104 Starfighter interceptor. Soon to be the holder of 46 world performance records, the J79 proved to be the ideal engine for the F4H-1.

US Navy design requirements remained vague throughout early 1955, possibly due to a lack of funds being available to give McDonnell approval to cut metal on the first prototype. Indeed, it seemed to be challenging the manufacturer to come up with new ideas for the fighter, rather than signing off on what McDonnell had created. Barkey's team responded with a succession of interchangeable noses for different missions, featuring Mk 12 20mm guns, 2.75-in. unguided rockets, electronic countermeasures (ECM) equipment or cameras. Nose sections were to be switched in a few hours aboard the carrier, thereby changing the aircraft's role.

In April 1955 it finally became clear that the F4H-1 was to be a fleet defence fighter, and three months later McDonnell was contracted to produce two prototypes and five pre-production aircraft. With the US Navy having decided against using the design in the ground attack role, McDonnell was instructed to delete all the pylon hard-points except for the centreline station. Luckily for the jet's long-term future, it was too late to remove all the AH-1 pylons, however, so seven hard-points remained. Other crucial decisions gave the aircraft an all-missile armament, two seats and two engines. Twin engines would become a McDonnell trademark, with the only exception being the disastrous F3H.

With J79s, the F4H-1 would have the speed to intercept fast, incoming bombers (US Navy planners feared the possibility of a supersonic Soviet B-58 equivalent

F-4B PHANTOM II

58ft 3.75in.

16ft 3in.

38ft 5in.

attacking the fleet with stand-off missiles) and the power to carry a heavy missile armament and a second crewman to operate the radar. McDonnell designers were also aware that the MiG-19 interceptor, capable of Mach 1.5, had flown in September 1953. Extra fuel would be carried in the wide fuselage to preserve range requirements, and one engine could be shut down for fuel economy. With so much power available, additional equipment and external weapons could be added in future without the usual need to calculate what effect every pound would have on the aircraft's performance, as had been the case with previous underpowered fighters.

The addition of a second cockpit went against most "fighter pilot" philosophy of the time. The US Navy only had one two-seat fighter, the lumbering F3D Skyknight with weighty nightfighting radar gear aboard. However, both McDonnell and the US Navy insisted that the F4H-1 needed a complex radar fit (ultimately the AN/APQ-72), and a separate operator for it.

In June 1956, following successful tests, the Raytheon Sparrow III semi-active radar-guided medium range air-to-air missile was made the primary armament. The Raytheon Aero 1A missile fire-control system was added the following April, at which point the design's 20mm cannon were deleted. Missiles were lighter than guns, and they could also be fired from a considerable distance without the crew having to run the risk of being shot down by the bomber's defensive guns. Finally, the missile's semi-active nature reduced the cockpit workload for the crew since the weapon itself would take over the interception task once it was supplied with initial guidance data.

For a three-hour patrol at the outer limits of a carrier battlegroup's defensive perimeter, the F4H-1 was required to carry eight missiles. In the event of an interception, these were to be salvoed in pairs from a "snap up" supersonic climb from medium altitude.

As the design progressed, it moved further from its F3H Demon origins. Although the wing area was similar in size, the flying surfaces themselves were thinner in width to permit supersonic flight. An extended 'saw-tooth' folding outer section was also added in an effort to prevent "pitch-up" at high speeds. In order to keep the main section of the wing (which was built around a massive forging that lent the aircraft much of its strength) as flat as possible, the outer wings were given 12 degrees dihedral to lend stability when the aircraft rolled. This was combined with a 23-degree anhedral "droop" in the one-piece stabilator, which was the best match for roll stability, and a very large vertical stabiliser.

A new material in the form of honeycomb panels sealed in a metal "sandwich" was used for the outer stabilator and rudder. Then-new titanium metal was also incorporated into the F4H-1, with the jet's lower rear fuselage (which was exposed to the fierce heat of the J79s in afterburner) being clad in it because of its heat-resistant qualities.

A major innovation for any fighter was the first ever set of variable geometry air intakes to provide smooth airflow to the engines. Their leading edge configuration was modified during flight-testing, and they ultimately proved vital in guaranteeing the success of the J79s in combat flying situations.

With the US Navy requiring the first two of 16 prototypes and pre-production aircraft to be ready by September 1958, McDonnell moved ahead fast on the F4H-1 once contracts had been signed. Taxiing tests were commenced by test pilot Robert C. Little on May 16, 1958 and the first prototype (BuNo 142259) made its maiden flight 11 days later. On June 2 the aircraft reached Mach 1.68 and 50,000ft, and soon afterwards James McDonnell decided to call his new product Phantom II, rather than "Satan" or "Ghost" as his employees preferred.

At a time when the US Navy was striving to preserve its nuclear strike capability in the face of a growing USAF monopoly, the F4H-1's Lear AJB-3/3A bomb delivery system allowed the jet to "toss" a Mk 10 nuclear weapon. It also gave the aircraft a limited conventional bombing capability, and this was to prove crucial during the Vietnam War.

For the F4H-1's primary air-to-air role, development of the Sparrow missile continued. Amongst the systems created was an explosive ejection device that separated the missile from its semi-recessed well beneath the fighter's fuselage without damaging the weapon's sensitive control circuits.

Targets were to be detected by a Westinghouse AN/APQ-50 radar, already used in basic form in the F4D Skyray and F2H-3 Banshee, via a 24-inch reflector dish that was originally intended for fitment to McDonnell's initial choice of radar. The latter was a system developed by Autonetics, but the US Navy chose the tried and tested AN/APQ-50 instead. Westinghouse demanded a considerably larger 32-inch dish to give its radar adequate range, and this in turn required the creation of a much wider nose radome than had been fitted to any previous fighter. The Brunswick Company produced a suitable fibreglass model (tested by the fifth pre-production aircraft), which had to be mounted with sufficient "droop" for the pilot to see over the nose when landing.

Up-rated and fitted with the appreciably larger 32-inch dish, the AN/APQ-50 morphed into the AN/APQ-72. The latter used an APA-128 continuous-wave injection system that locked the main antenna in the general direction of the enemy aircraft and created a beam of radar for the missile to "ride" as its own continuous-wave miniature radar sought the target. It was up to the Radar Intercept Officer (RIO) sat behind the pilot to create a three-dimensional interpretation of the luminescent blobs on his screen that would in turn ensure that the AIM-7 Sparrow was launched at the optimum point in the interception profile.

The F4H-1's secondary armament, the AIM-9 Sidewinder, was a US Navy project from the outset. Each missile cost half the price of a Sparrow, and if the F4H-1 pilot's first head-on attack with the latter was unsuccessful, he could swing round behind his adversary for a heat-seeking Sidewinder attack from astern. Initially, McDonnell fitted a small ACF Electronics AAA-4 infrared seeker in a six-inch bullet fairing beneath the F4H-1's main radome to search a wider sky spectrum for infrared targets for the Sidewinder's narrow detection cone. However, the missile's acquisition capability improved rapidly, and the little-used AAA-4 was soon deleted.

With its original Stanley ejection seats replaced by heavier, more expensive, British Martin-Baker models, the rear canopy raised to give the RIO some sort of external view and refinements to the air intakes, the F4H-1 completed three years of testing and was ready for fleet service by late 1961. Seventy-two F4H-1s were initially ordered, with alternate aircraft in the batch having control columns and rudder pedals fitted in their rear cockpits so as to facilitate pilot training in the early stages of the aircraft.

By then the McDonnell design had also seen off the challenge posed by the Vought F8U-3. The US Navy had been keen to ensure that it had a viable alternate fighter available should the F4H-1 programme fail to live up to expectations (thus avoiding a repeat of the F3H-1 debacle), so Vought had been given the chance to compete with the Phantom II through the fail-safe development of its excellent F8U Crusader. Although the F8U-3 was an all new aeroplane that demonstrated superior performance to the F4H-1 in many areas, and was well supported by Naval Aviators in the fleet who had nothing but praise for the F8U-1/2, the US Navy opted for the security of two seats, two engines and more versatile armament capability.

Record flight attempts with the F4H-1 began in October 1959, and US Navy Board of Inspection and Survey trials had been completed using eight pre-production airframes by the end of 1960. The Phantom II's record flights – particularly the eight new "time to climb" Project *High Jump* flights in early 1962 – demonstrated to both friend and foe alike that the F-4B (as the F4H-1 had become under the combined service designation system adopted in September 1962) was a world-beating interceptor.

Fleet squadron training commenced in February 1961 with VF-121 at Miramar, in California, followed by VF-101 at Oceana, in Virginia. The latter unit trained three Atlantic Fleet squadrons in just 18 months from July 1961.

By then the USAF was showing a keen interest in the fighter to replace its F-105 Thunderchief, and it eventually received 583 F-4Cs from late 1963 – this variant was essentially little more than a slightly modified F-4B. The US Marine Corps also ordered the F-4B and the dedicated RF-4B tactical reconnaissance variant, which first flew in

The F-4J first deployed with VF-84 and VF-41 in February 1967, and it entered the war with VF-33 and VF-102 during the first Westpac cruise made by USS *America* (CVA-66) in April 1968. Capt Bill Knutson, then with VF-33, thought that the F-4J was "more stable than the F-4B. The extra thrust was great for ACM, and when the radar worked it provided a great increase in combat capability with its look-down ability. Best of all, it was super to bring aboard a carrier, and the large tyres greatly reduced blow-outs on landing". Here, F-4J-40-MC BuNo 157257 of VF-114 is launched from USS *Kitty Hawk* (CVA-63) on yet another CAP sortie in early 1971. This aircraft was later converted into an F-4S. (McDonnell Douglas via John Harty)

March 1965. Shortly after the aircraft had entered frontline service with all three operators, the McDonnell team began work on improved versions for the US Navy/Marine Corps (F-4J) and the USAF (F-4D) that shared many parts under the government's "commonality" principle.

First flown on May 27, 1966, the F-4J remained in production until April 1972. It shared the F-4D's beefed-up undercarriage and, under Project *Shoehorn*, the aircraft (along with many F-4Bs) was fitted with the AN/APR-30/32 radar-homing and warning system (RHAWS) to give the crew timely alerts

on incoming surface-to-air missiles (SAMs). The jet's new AN/AWG-10 fire control system was also more effective at managing air-to-air missile engagements and, for the first time, provided the crew with effective look-down radar capability and built-in testing. In 1973 further solid-state additions and a digital computer in the AWG-10A signalled the beginning of a new generation of fighter avionics.

The lack of a gun in US Navy F-4s was a frequent source of dissatisfaction and missed MiG kills, but putting a Vulcan gun in the nose, as had been done with the USAF's F-4E, placed the aircraft's centre of gravity too far forward to allow the jet to safely undertake carrier operations.

Updates to the F-4B were provided from June 1972 when the first of 228 surviving airframes were "re-lifed" as F-4Ns during Project *Bee Line* – modified aircraft were returned to the fleet from February 1973. As part of the update they were given Sanders AN/ALQ-126 defensive ECM system, a Honeywell AN/AVG-8 helmet-mounted visual target acquisition system (VTAS) and other improvements. These aircraft were followed from July 1977 by 248 re-manufactured F-4Js, which emerged with similar updates as F-4S Phantom IIs. Most also received leading-edge slats like those fitted to the USAF's F-4Es in an effort to improve manoeuvrability and low-speed handling.

MiG-17

OKB Mikoyan-Gurevich had produced the USSR's first jet fighter, the MiG-9, in 1946 using a conventional straight-winged airframe and engines based on German samples discovered when Soviet troops captured the BMW and Junkers Jumo factories in 1945. Two copied BMW 003 turbojets enabled the hastily produced fighter to reach 467 knots, carrying an enormous 57mm cannon and two 23mm guns in its nose. Production aircraft, with one 37mm and two 23mm guns (as in the MiG-17) were ordered immediately, but problems with the early jet soon became obvious.

VF-96's "Showtime 608" carries two AIM-7Es and two AIM-9Bs in typical BARCAP configuration during the unit's first of four war cruises with USS *Enterprise* (CVAN-65). This initial deployment ran from October 1965 through to June 1966. The squadron's tiger-stripe tips on the wings and fin-cap helped pilots with formation keeping, and were repeated in different colours on the mounts of many other F-4 squadrons. Aside from its missiles, this aircraft also carries a centreline tank, which was a vital, but sometimes problematic, external store. Tank nosecones occasionally collapsed during high-speed or high-g flight, causing severe flight control problems. Before a combat engagement, the tank had to be jettisoned in straight and level flight at a set low speed (depending on whether it still contained fuel or not) or else it would rear up and hit the aircraft's underside. A momentary positive 1g climb helped with separation. (via Peter Mersky)

MiG-17F

36ft 5in.

2047

12ft 5in.

31ft 7in.

OPPOSITE
MiG-17F "Fresco-C" 2047 was one of two examples that were modified with braking parachutes to operate from the forward airstrip at Gat for anti-shipping strikes. They could also carry two PROSAB 250kg bombs. Top MiG-17 ace Nguyen Van Bay and his wingman Le Xuan Di (in aircraft 2002) took off from Gat during the early evening of April 19, 1972 to attack ships that were shelling coastal targets from close offshore. On his third pass at the destroyer USS *Higbee* (DD-806), Le Xuan Di knocked out the ship's aft 5-in. turret. Luckily, its 12-man gun crew had evacuated the turret minutes earlier while a jammed shell was hosed down. Van Bay caused slight damage to the cruiser USS *Oklahoma City* (CLG-5). Terrier missiles were launched at the MiGs from the destroyer USS *Sterett* (DDG-31), one of which missed its target. However, a second allegedly destroyed a MiG-17 — one of three that US Navy observers reportedly saw in the vicinity of the vessels. 2047 was subsequently displayed in Hanoi with Van Bay's seven fading aerial kill symbols beneath the cockpit.

At speeds above 270 knots it was impossible for the pilot to bail out as there was no ejection seat. When all three guns were fired at altitudes above 24,000ft, both engines usually surged and flamed out. The lack of airbrakes, cockpit pressurisation and engine fire-suppression equipment were also symptoms of Premier Josef Stalin's desire to push the aircraft into service too quickly. Indeed, the MiG-9's only real advantage over contemporary piston-engined designs was a higher top speed.

Typically for a Soviet design, a large number of prototypes were built around the basic MiG-9 to test two-seat configuration, different armament fits, nose-mounted radar, rocket power and, in 1947, one of the 25 Rolls-Royce Nene centrifugal turbojet engines sold to the USSR by a British Labour Party-sponsored trade delegation in 1946. Prior to the sale, Artem Mikoyan and engine designer Vladimir Klimov had actually visited England to study the engine. Considerably more advanced, and reliable, than the copied German turbojets that powered the MiG-9, the Nenes were swiftly reverse engineered for Soviet production as the RD-45 (later Klimov VK-1).

Ultimately, the Nene-powered MiG-9 was never completed, for OKB Mikoyan-Gurevich had turned its attention to a far more exciting design by early 1946. The appearance of its MiG-15 in the skies over war torn Korea almost five years later was as big a shock to the air arms of the United Nations as the arrival of the Mitsubishi A6M Zero-sen had been to the Allies in the Pacific War in December 1941.

In March 1946 Stalin had challenged his aircraft designers to create a new fighter that was far in advance of the types produced immediately post-war, demanding an interceptor with a top speed of 620mph, a ceiling of 46,000ft and rough-field operating capability The lack of a suitable engine was solved by the Nene copy, and the crucial, German-inspired, swept wing was chosen after wind-tunnel tests.

The MiG-9's missing ejection seat, airbrakes and cockpit pressurisation were remedied and hydraulic boost was added for the first time to the ailerons in an otherwise mechanical flight control system. The detachable rear fuselage, inspired by Lockheed's contemporary F-80 Shooting Star, gave quick access to the engine, while a clever gun tray (like the one subsequently fitted to the Hawker Hunter) housing all three weapons, and their ammunition, could be lowered on a built-in hoist. The choice of guns was, once again, a single N-37 37mm cannon with 40 rounds and two NS-23s 23mm cannons with 80 rounds apiece. Two 260-litre slipper-type drop tanks under the wings added enough fuel to give the MiG-15 a maximum overload range of 1,100 miles.

Like its predecessor, the new fighter was rushed into production and experimental sub-variants proliferated. One tested the faster-firing NR-23 cannon, while others had radar noses, twin seats (ultimately built as the MiG-15UTI, examples of which comprised almost half of the jet's total 5,000+ production run), ground attack pylons for ordnance (MiG-15ISh) and the afterburning VK-1F engine that would subsequently be used in the MiG-17. During the Korean War, the improved MiG-15bis flown by Soviet, North Korean and Chinese pilots demonstrated superior climb and turn rates and a higher operational ceiling than the USAF's F-86E Sabre. Against straight-winged types like the F-80, F-84, F9F and Meteor, the MiG had every advantage.

When aimed accurately (fortunately a fairly rare occurrence), its heavy, slow-firing cannon, designed to be used against bombers, could hit targets at longer range than the Sabre's six 0.50-in. machine guns. Despite this, the much better trained USAF pilots, many of whom had World War II fighter experience to draw upon, used their more reliable and better-equipped fighters to score a kill/loss ratio of at least 4-to-1 against MiG-15 pilots.

The MiG-17, on which design work began in 1949, was intended to correct any problems revealed during the MiG-15's combat debut. Production was delayed by the pressure to manufacture more MiG-15s for combat, and the new fighter did not enter service in the USSR until October 1952 – by which time the appreciably faster MiG-19 was on the verge of commencing flight testing.

Referred to originally as the MiG-15bis45, the revised design changed the MiG-15's 35-degree constant wing sweepback to a compound 45-degree angle (like the North American F-100 Super Sabre) up to the mid-span, and 42 degrees for the rest of the wing. This was called a "sickle" sweep, and it was less radical than the "crescent" wing used on the Handley Page Victor bomber, for example.

Like the MiG-15 "Fagot" (NATO reporting name), the new design was to be a lightweight, simple and reliable machine that would continue the tradition of the "samolyot-soldaht" ("soldier aircraft"). While using much of the MiG-15's structure, the new design sought to remedy some of its shortcomings. The new wing improved the lift-to-drag ratio and overcame the MiG-15's tendency to dip a wingtip unexpectedly at high speed because the structure was not stiff enough to maintain aerodynamic symmetry under high wing loads. Flight controls, avionics and armament remained virtually unchanged, but the tail section *was* altered, with a larger vertical tail and a 45-degree rather than 40-degree sweep to the horizontal surfaces.

The MiG-15bis45 (SI-1 prototype) crashed on March 17, 1950, probably as a result of "flutter" tearing off the horizontal tail. Aileron control reversal at high speed due to a lack of wing stiffness (a common problem in early swept-wing jets) was also discovered and remedied.

With so many changes to the MiG-15 design it was clear that a new designation was needed, and the aircraft became known as the MiG-17 during its acceptance trials in

the summer of 1951. The fighter was ordered into production before those trials had been completed, and service evaluation began at Krymskaya air base, in Crimea, before year-end. Shortly afterwards it was given the NATO reporting name "Fresco-A".

Soviet pilots found the aircraft stable, but slightly heavier on the controls than the MiG-15. The airbrakes from the latter soon proved to be too small, the undercarriage brakes inadequate and the elevator actuators underpowered. Test pilots also advocated a stability augmentation system as used in Western fighters, but none was available. However, pilots did get a safer ejection seat with a Martin-Baker style protective face curtain and leg restraints in 1953. A clear-vision canopy without the heavy rear frame was designed, but the cheaper option of a rear-view periscope was installed in production MiG-17Fs. After the capture of a USAF F-86A Sabre in 1951 in Korea, Soviet engineers copied its optical gunsight and gun ranging radar, which subsequently appeared as the ASP-4N gunsight and SRD-3 gun ranging radar in test-bed MiG-17s from October 1952. These systems were later introduced to production aircraft in modified form.

The most significant improvement came with the availability of the VK-1F afterburning engine, which was the first effective Soviet unit of its kind. The basic Nene-inspired VK-1A was at the limit of its development by 1951, and afterburning was the only way to increase the thrust output of the turbojet engine. In the MiG-17F (the "F" indicated 'afterburning' in both engine and aircraft designations), a modified rear fuselage accommodated the convergent-divergent engine nozzle and the fuel system was modified.

Testing showed that the new engine made supersonic flight just about possible in a shallow dive. It also doubled the fighter's rate of climb and made vertical manoeuvres during dogfights far easier to perform. It yielded little improvement in horizontal speed, however. Just short of Mach 1, the aircraft would suddenly pitch up and the available elevator stick forces were not enough to prevent this.

The need for an all-weather version of the MiG-17 meant that the second "Fresco-A" development aircraft (SP-2) was immediately used to test the "Korshun" radar in a bullet radome above the intake. From 1952 onwards, testing of the MiG-17P with an Izumrud RP-1M radar in place of the "Korshun" began, and this variant was eventually placed in production as the USSR's first lightweight radar-

When the first batch of MiG-17s was delivered to Noi Bai airfield on August 6, 1964, the type had already been in production for 13 years. Its first combat mission had been flown in July 1953, when Soviet air force MiG-17s shot down a USAF RB-50 reconnaissance aircraft near Vladivostok. The "Fresco" was the USSR's mainstay fighter from the mid-1950s onwards, and it remained in limited use with Third World air arms into the 1990s thanks to its tough simplicity, which made it ideal for inexperienced client air forces. (via Dr István Toperczer)

Cdr John Nash, one of the original *Topgun* team pilots, flew the MiG-17 and MiG-21 both with Project *Have Drill* and as manager of the *Have Idea* programme, matching the aircraft against a range of US Navy tactical jets. In his opinion, "flown by a proficient air combat pilot, it was very difficult to beat. It could enter a 6g turn doing about 375 knots and would not lose more than 10 knots in a 360-degree turn at full power". Shenyang J-5 "Fresco-C" 2011 was once the mount of Ngo Duc Mai, who claimed two and three shared victories. The J-5 differed in detail from the Soviet-built MiG-17, the former, for example, having a single brake line rather than two for each main undercarriage leg. (Dr István Toperczer)

equipped interceptor – the "Fresco-B". This was followed in May 1953 by the "Fresco-D" (MiG-17PF), which received the more powerful Izumrud RP-2 from December 1955. The installation of a search radar did not free the MiG-17PF from reliance upon Ground Control Interception (GCI), however.

MiG-19

The MiG-19's importance in the evolution of MiG fighters far outweighed its brief Soviet air force (VVS) career. Skilled MiG-17 pilots were sometimes able to make brief supersonic dashes, but a genuine supersonic fighter was needed. As early as June 1950 Josef Stalin had told the heads of Russia's aircraft industry that he wanted a twin-engined fighter that could be manufactured both as a radar-equipped all-weather interceptor and as a supersonic tactical fighter. Clearly, he was well ahead of Robert S. McNamara's 1960s ideas of "commonality" in the USA.

Mikoyan saw that an increase in wing sweep had made his MiG-17 faster than the MiG-15, so he opted for a 55-degree sweep in the SM-2 prototype that was to pioneer Soviet supersonic flight. With a high T-tail, two Mikulin AM-5F engines and tail surfaces swept back to match the wing, the aircraft was barely supersonic. It also exhibited severe stability problems. The SM-2 was followed by the SM-9/1, which featured a fuselage-mounted tailplane, two afterburning AM-9B engines and three NR-23 cannons.

On its first flight on January 5, 1954, the new fighter exhibited vastly improved handling over the SM-2, and it was soon making regular supersonic flights. Indeed, tests showed it to be 205 knots faster than the MiG-17 at 32,800ft, and capable of attaining a ceiling of 51,500ft – 3,000ft higher than the "Fresco". Designated the MiG-19 for service production, the aircraft was ordered for the VVS on February 17, 1954. Testing continued with the SM-9/2 and SM-9/3, proving the effectiveness of the "slab" tailplane layout and introducing a spoiler system to improve lateral control, as well as many refinements to the flight controls and their servos.

The SM-9/3 – dubbed "3 Red" – tested the production armament of three NR-30 30mm cannon, whose combined weight of fire (40lbs per second) was twice that of three NR-23s. Like the MiG-17, the SM-9/3 also had two underwing hardpoints to carry a 550lb bomb each. This was the pattern aircraft for MiG-19S "Farmer-C" production, with RD-9B engines (one of the first powerplants credited to designer Sergei K. Tumansky) each developing 7,164lbs thrust – almost twice that of the MiG-17's VK-1F engine. Some gun-gas ingestion engine surges occurred when the nose cannon was fired, and it was found that the engines flamed out in a spin.

While the aircraft prepared to enter service, OKB MiG worked on its galaxy of experimental sub-variants, of which the MiG-19P and MiG-19PM were each produced in greater numbers than the MiG-19S (443, 369 and 317 units, respectively). Production of the former began in 1957 after only two years of MiG-19S manufacturing. Both sub-types were designed to use K-5M semi-active, air-to-air missiles as Soviet designers followed their Western counterparts into the missile age. Four were carried on underwing pylons, and they were guided by the fighter's RP-5 Izumrud-2 radar. Two NR-30 cannon were retained, but only in the MiG-19P. Performance suffered from the drag of the missiles, and the flight control system in the MiG-19P/PM proved to be less reliable than that fitted in the MiG-19S.

The majority of MiG-19 production took place in China rather than in the USSR. Following on from its licence-production of the MiG-17F (Shenyang J-5), China began to make the MiG-19 (Shenyang J-6) in 1957. Indeed, production totalling around 4,000 MiG-19S, P and PM units continued until 1986. Quality control suffered during high-volume production, particularly after China temporarily rejected Soviet help in building early examples, but the aircraft gradually evolved into a more reliable machine than its Russian forebear.

Although the MiG-19 offered important performance improvements over the "Fresco", it had already been beaten into VPAF service by the superior MiG-21 by some four years. The 925th FR was the sole VPAF MiG-19 unit, and it operated from Yen Bai – a poorly equipped, one runway air base that accommodated the squadron from February 1969. Many of the regiment's pilots had already received MiG-21 training, and nine had transitioned to the "Farmer" by April. In this staged photograph, the unit's commanding officer instructs his 16 pilots in dogfighting techniques while a second squad gets another lecture further down the flightline. (VPAF Museum via Dr István Toperczer)

TECHNICAL SPECIFICATIONS

F-4B PHANTOM II

The Phantom II's interceptor role was obvious externally through its large radome and long-range missile armament. The radome housed a Westinghouse AN/APQ-72 I/J-band interception radar with a 32-inch dish, operated by the RIO from the aircraft's rear cockpit. Although reliant upon thermionic valves, which reduced reliability in frontline conditions when operating from a carrier, the radar was long-ranging in detecting targets when functioning correctly. The RIO then used the aircraft's APA-157

VF-92 F-4B "Silver Kite 201" commences its catapult stroke along *Enterprise's* waist cat four during the unit's second combat tour in March 1966. The extending nose-gear leg, blown flaps and slats and 34,000lbs of thrust were all needed to supplement the massive power of the ship's catapult in launching 50,000lbs of Phantom II off the flightdeck. Pilots were instructed to "move the throttles outboard into the afterburner detent. When satisfied that the aircraft is ready, give an exaggerated left-hand salute to the catapult officer while maintaining aft stick with the right hand". (McDonnell-Douglas)

illuminator to guide an AIM-7D/E Sparrow for head-on attacks at a range of 12+ miles, or stern attacks at up to four miles. Four AIM-7Es could be carried, and they were most successful when launched head-on at beyond visual range against a clear-sky background. The "secondary" armament (often the most effective in Vietnam) was the AIM-9B Sidewinder infrared-seeking missile, which could be used with more success against manoeuvring targets at shorter ranges than the Sparrow.

Powering the F-4B were two of world's most successful jet engines – the reliable General Electric J79-GE-8A, each developing 17,000lbs of thrust in full afterburner. They were supplied with fuel from two internal wing tanks housing 638 US gallons, six internal fuel cells containing 1356 US gallons and up to three drop tanks with another 1340 US gallons. In-flight refuelling was also possible via a retractable probe to feed the thirsty J79s with their basic one mile per gallon consumption.

The considerable weight of the F-4B's engines, fuel and armament gave it a wing loading factor of 81 – almost twice that of the MiG-17 – which considerably reduced its manoeuvrability at speeds below 350 knots. Its flight controls were innovative, comprising inboard ailerons (coupled with spoilers above the wings), an all-moving stabilator and a powerful rudder. All controls were managed via a stability augmentation system. A total of 649 F-4Bs were produced.

F-4J PHANTOM II

The first of 522 F-4Js was flown on May 27, 1966. It had the wider wheels and strengthened undercarriage legs of the USAF's F-4C, a seventh fuselage fuel cell and a larger APG-59 radar to feed the sophisticated AN/AWG-10 fire-control system. This pulse Doppler system gave much improved air-to-ground capability, and it enabled the radar to "see" airborne targets better against a background of terrain. The F-4B's largely unused AAA-4 infrared sensor was deleted from beneath the radome. J79-GE-10 engines developing 17,900lbs of thrust, with revised afterburner nozzles, were installed. The combination of a slotted leading edge to the stabilator (also retro-

An F-4J carrier approach commenced at 20 miles out from an altitude of 5,000ft, with the aircraft descending at a rate of 2,000ft per minute. Gear and flaps were extended at ten miles out and 195 knots. At the six-mile "gate", a 600ft altitude was maintained until the controller called "commence landing descent", or the pilot sighted the "meatball" visual landing aid. Descent then reduced from 500ft a minute at one mile to 300ft a minute at half-a-mile. All approaches and landings were tele-recorded and graded from "OK" to "Cut Pass" (dangerous), with the latter having consequences for the pilot's future career prospects. As VF-21 pilot Cdr Dave Daniels recalled, "You could talk all day about being the world's greatest MiG killer, but if you couldn't consistently plant the aeroplane back aboard the ship, day or night, right in front of the No 3 wire, all that talk didn't go far". The MiG kill on the splitter plate of this VF-31 F-4J, landing aboard USS Saratoga (CVA-60), in early 1973, was actually scored by Cdr Sam Flynn and Lt Bill John in BuNo 157307 "Bandwagon 106". (US Navy via C. Moggeridge)

F-4B/J PHANTOM II MISSILE ARMAMENT VIEWS

Although the F-4 was designed to carry four AIM-7E Sparrow III missiles beneath its fuselage for the interception mission, the US Navy tended increasingly to hang only two AIM-7s in the rear fuselage wells and rely on four AIM-9s mounted in pairs on Aero 3B underwing launchers. This reflected a general preference for the more reliable Sidewinder, and it helped to rectify the F-4's nose-heavy catapult launch posture. The AIM-9 was a US Navy project, produced in B, C, D and G models during the war with increasing reliability and tracking ability. AIM-7s were sometimes carried on the inner wing pylons early in the war. The centreline fuel tank had to be dropped before Sparrows could be fired from the fuselage stations.

As the aircraft touched down, the pilot advanced the throttles to full military power until it was clear that the tailhook had made a safe arrestment. Power was then cut to idle, the tailhook was raised and the Phantom II rolled back a little to release the arresting cable. With brakes applied, the wing-fold pin release was operated and toggle switch moved to the FOLD position. The aircraft was marshalled to its tie-down position before the crew could climb out. Jury struts were installed to support the folded wing. This F-4J belonged to VF-84, which made a single war cruise with F-4Bs in 1965. (US Navy via C. Moggeridge)

fitted to many F-4B/Ns) and locking the inboard leading-edge wing flaps in the "up" position improved low-speed handling.

Like the MiG-17, the F-4 was in some ways "overbuilt", but the naval fighter required its beefy structure to cope with the enormous stresses of deck landings and catapult launches. A massive tailhook and folding outer wing panels were further, necessary, additional weight. Many F-4Bs were retrofitted with AN/APR-30 RHAW equipment, housed in a distinctive revised fin-cap. Twelve were delivered as F-4Gs (ten of which went to VF-213), equipped with data-link sets in part of the No 1 fuel tank area, which allowed night and all-weather "hands off" carrier landings and an automatic flow of information between the F-4G, airborne early warning aircraft and other ships for remote-control interceptions. Too complex in practice, most of the equipment was removed and the aircraft reverted to the F-4B designation.

MiG-17 (VPAF USE ONLY)

Developed from the Korean War-vintage MiG-15, the MiG-17 was essentially a first-generation jet fighter. Its engine (crucially featuring afterburner) and armament came directly from the MiG-15, and were built into a three-foot longer fuselage. The MiG-17 had an improved instrument panel, however, as well as a safer ejection seat that allowed the pilot to abandon his aircraft at altitudes as low as 800ft.

It was considered to be inferior to "second generation" supersonic types like the F-105 and F-4, but its light weight gave the MiG-17 the great advantage of being able to turn in combat far more tightly than either American fighter. This duly meant that pilots flying the "Fresco" could employ the jet's heavy gun armament at close quarters. The Phantom II's all-missile armament could not be used at less than 700ft range, and "minimum range" safety requirements pushed this distance out to around 3,000ft in practice. The MiG's cannon were effective at ranges from zero up to 5,000ft, and although the aircraft only carried enough ammunition for a five-second burst of fire, a single strike by 37mm shell that weighed in at 750 grams could easily disable a US fighter.

Lacking radar or advanced avionics, the MiG-17 pilot relied on accurate guidance from GCI in order to get within firing range of his target. Good visibility in daylight conditions was also essential.

MiG-17 "FRESCO-A"

As the first mass-produced version of the MiG-21, Some of the earliest jets delivered to the VPAF were "Fresco-A' models, which differed from the MiG-17F in having no afterburner and smaller airbrakes, fitted lower on the rear fuselage. Maximum speed was only about 30mph less than the afterburning MiG-17F at a typical 16,000ft combat altitude, but rate of climb was roughly half that of the MiG-17F.

MiG-17F "FRESCO-C"

This was the main production variant of the MiG-17 following limited manufacture of the MiG-17 "Fresco-A". An afterburner was added to the Klimov VK-1F engine, boosting its performance by more than 600lbs static thrust. This in turn increased the fighter's service ceiling by 1,000ft and doubled its rate of climb. The "Fresco-C" had hydraulic airbrakes of increased area, which could be deflected to 55 degrees to force an enemy fighter to overshoot in combat.

The wing was an improved version of that fitted to the MiG-15, with a thinner aerofoil to increase speed, greater sweep-back and area and three "fences" to control boundary layer air. It contained no fuel tanks, unlike the F-4's wing, making it less vulnerable in combat.

The MiG-17F's internal fuel capacity was only 374 gallons (little more than one of the F-4's external wing tanks), and a further 176 gallons could be carried in two drop tanks. Refuelling was by the gravity method via two filler caps behind the cockpit, with a third at the side of the rear fuselage for the 35-gallon tank that was located beneath the engine exhaust pipe.

In all respects the maintenance of the aircraft was very simple, using basic tools and lubricant cans. The single hydraulic system powered the landing gear, flaps, airbrakes and aileron actuating mechanism. Two pneumatic systems actuated the wheel brakes, pressurised the cockpit and charged the guns, as well as providing a back-up system to lower the undercarriage and flaps. The entire rear section of the fuselage could be detached at a point just forward of the wing trailing edge, allowing full access for engine maintenance.

Early production J-5 "Fresco-A" 2614 was photographed on display within the Nha Trang air base museum in the markings it bore for action in 1967. The fighter has the smaller airbrakes fitted to early production aircraft and no afterburner. A number of different airbrake locations were tested on prototype "Fresco-As", including positions just aft of the wing. Pilots found that the MiG-17 was very manoeuvrable, but heavier on the controls than the MiG-15s that many of them had flown in training. The gun camera is visible above the intake.
(Dr István Toperczer)

The forward fuselage section, which was very similar to the MiG-15's, contained the pressurised cockpit, two avionics bays, the No 1 fuel tank and a weapons bay.

To simplify re-arming and maintenance of the MiG-17's guns, the three cannon, their ammunition boxes and pneumatic charging mechanisms were built into a tray that could be lowered from the fuselage by its own built-in winch. Simple refuelling methods and this "palletised" gun system meant that the aircraft could be turned around in 20 minutes and sent back into action.

The Nudel'man N-37D 37mm cannon had been in Soviet service since 1946. Designed for bomber interceptors, it could fire 400 rounds per minute, although no more than 40 were normally carried. It developed powerful recoil action, which was used to recharge the gun, and the weapon's waste gases, discharged close to the engine intake, could cause the powerplant to surge dangerously. On the left hand side of the gun bay were two Nudel'man-Rikhter NR-23 single-barrel 23mm cannon capable of firing more than 650 rounds per minute, with 80 rounds carried per gun. This weapon was installed in a wide variety of Soviet aircraft and licence-manufactured in China.

Together, the three guns could deliver more than 70lbs of shells in a two-second burst – twice the weight of fire of the F-8 Crusader's four 20mm cannon. However, gun harmonisation was often inadequate, and a primitive gunsight, together with aircraft vibration and stability problems at high speed, reduced the effect of the slow-firing cannon. US pilots reported many occurrences of inaccurate shooting by MiG-17 pilots, even at close range.

Powering the MiG-17 was an engine that originated in 1944 as the Rolls-Royce Nene, used in the British Sea Hawk and Attacker fighters. The Soviets produced 39,000 unlicensed copies, and it remained in production in China until 1979. Simple and cheap to build, the smokeless Nene (designated the Klimov VK-1F in the USSR) had a single centrifugal compressor and a single-stage axial turbine. Klimov added a short afterburner with a two-position nozzle, although this took more than five seconds to light up and could only be used for three minutes continuously. Engine acceleration was, therefore, generally slow. Despite this, the VK-1F allowed the MiG-17 to maintain a tight turn at lower airspeeds better than US fighters.

Flying controls were conventional ailerons, elevators and a rudder, all operated by mechanical rods and cranks, with electrically operated trim tabs. The lack of powered

This MiG-17F's Soviet origins are evident from the Cyrillic stencilling below the windshield. Seen in the late summer of 1964, this aircraft has an early type of cartridge-fired ejection seat. Later deliveries had a seat with metal stabilising fins on the head-rest and a face curtain to protect the pilot at ejection speeds up to 525 knots. American flyers were surprised to note that their adversaries used square parachute canopies, often with the national flag attached to the canopy or seat pack to deter ground fire from trigger-happy militia who might mistake them for a "Yankee Air Pirate". (Zoltán Pintér via Dr István Toperczer)

MiG-17F GUNS

The MiG-17's armament was essentially carried over from the MiG-15, providing a brief but heavy punch. A single 37mm Nudel'man N-37D gun with 40 rounds fired massive 26.5-ounce projectiles at a rate of 400 shells per minute with a muzzle velocity of 2,263ft/sec. A single hit could cripple an enemy fighter, but excessive recoil made the weapon hard to aim and gun gases could cause engine surges. Two Nudel'man-Rikhter NR-23 (Norinco Type 23 in Chinese J-5 aircraft) cannon were paired on the starboard side. This short-recoil 23mm gun fired up to 650 rounds per minute at the same muzzle velocity as the N-37D, and its projectiles (80 per gun) weighed seven ounces each.

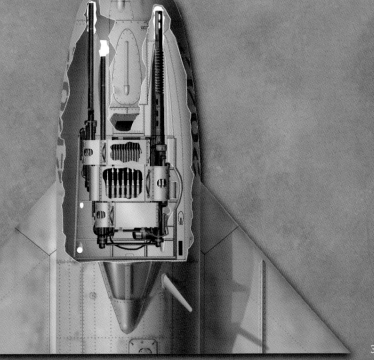

Re-arming and servicing the MiG-17's three cannon was simplified by winching down the guns and their ammunition boxes – the shaped fairings covering the guns also hinged downwards to ease access. American pilots in their combat reports often commented on the flame and smoke visible around the MiG's nose when the guns fired, as well as the "flaming golf ball" appearance of their large shells in flight. The 37mm weapon could destroy a target at 5,000ft, but VPAF pilots preferred to engage at much closer ranges. At the other end of the aircraft, the engine's uneven flickering afterburner flame could be mistaken for combat damage. (VPAF Museum via Dr István Toperczer)

control augmentation, fitted to US fighters, made the controls very heavy to operate, even with the unusually long control column to provide leverage. At 500 knots, stability and manoeuvrability became poor, and it was impossible for the pilot to pull the nose of the aircraft up to a steep angle. Above 595 knots at altitudes below 16,000ft, the airframe suffered from severe buffeting and the flying controls were rendered virtually useless.

The undercarriage typified the fighter's manual/mechanical systems. To lower it meant flipping a toggle switch, activating a pump and allowing hydraulic pressure to build up prior to pushing down a handle to lower and lock the undercarriage. The hydraulic pump then had to be switched off. In the F-4 the same procedure required a single switch movement.

The pilot's bubble canopy provided better visibility than that of later MiG-21s and many American fighters, although heavy frames, a bulky gunsight and a 2.5-in. thick bullet-proof glass windshield restricted forward vision. Chinese licence-built MiG-17Fs were designated Jianjiji-5s, or J-5s.

MiG-17PF "FRESCO-D"

Just ten radar-equipped MiG-17PF all-weather interceptors were supplied to the VPAF by the USSR in late 1965. They had a one-foot increase in fuselage length and a 496lb weight increase over the "Fresco-A", with consequent performance penalties. The nose accommodated the two antennas of the RP-5 Izumrud-2 "Scan Rod" fixed-range ranging radar in a radome mounted on the air intake splitter and in an extended lip directly above the intake itself. The gun camera was moved from this lip to the right side of the nose. To maintain balance, the solitary N-37 cannon was replaced by a third NR-23 gun. A handful of victories were claimed by 921st FR pilots that had been specially trained to fly the MiG-17PF.

MiG-19S "FARMER-C"/SHENYANG J-6

Having many innovations compared with the MiG-17, the MiG-19 was the Russian equivalent of the F-100 Super Sabre. Both aircraft were marginally capable of attaining supersonic speed in level flight, the MiG-19 having achieved this as the first Soviet supersonic interceptor in December 1952 – four months ahead of the F-100. Like the North American fighter, it initially suffered from control ability problems at high speeds. Both aircraft were given larger vertical tail surfaces to improve stability, and both featured one-piece stabilators instead of elevators – an innovation in Russia, hence the "S" in MiG-19S.

The MiG-19 was also the first Russian fighter to use axial-flow turbojets in the form of two Tumansky RD-9Bs, each yielding 7,164lbs of thrust, with a three-stage afterburner. They gave the aircraft a top speed of 903mph at 32,000ft and a service ceiling of 57,400ft.

The fighter's mid-position wing was drastically swept back at 55 degrees, with conventional ailerons and a single, large, fence per wing. Its wing load was a little higher than the MiG-17's at 51, but still far less than the F-4's. Internal fuel amounted to 477.3 gallons, supplemented by two 167-gallon drop tanks, to give a range of 1,243 miles. With a loaded weight some 6,000lbs heavier than the MiG-17F's, the aircraft could still reach 38,000ft in just 1.1 minutes – three times faster than the "Fresco".

Boasting a take-off run of 1,700ft when "clean", the MiG-19 could land in a 2,000ft run through the employment of a brake parachute (relocated from a ventral position to a fairing at the base of the fin in the J-6).

Maintenance of the MiG-17 did not require sophisticated tools or motorised service vehicles, as this photograph clearly demonstrates. This proved crucial to the VPAF, which was always short of skilled personnel. Frequent airfield attacks after the spring of 1967, and the effects of the humid climate on electronic equipment, considerably reduced "Fresco" serviceability by the end of Operation *Rolling Thunder*. The climate also quickly removed the poorly applied green or green/tan camouflage paint sprayed onto MiGs like 3012, seen here at Noi Bai. 2031 has an overall light grey paint scheme. (VPAF via Dr István Toperczer)

MiG-19S GUNS

Three 30mm NR-30 (Type 30 in Chinese licence manufacture) cannon formed the MiG-19S's basic armament. A scaled-up version of the MiG-17's NR-23, the NR-30's projectiles were twice as heavy, and fired at a rate in excess of 850 rounds per minute. The nose-mounted gun had up to 70 belt-fed projectiles in its magazine, and each wing gun had up to 73 rounds in ammunition trays that ran inside the leading edges. Initial gun charging was pneumatic, with recharging by recoil action. The MiG-19S wing pylons could carry 550lbs of bombs or ORO-57K 57mm rocket pods. Like the MiG-17, the "Farmer" had an AKS-5 or S-13 gun camera mounted in the intake lip.

The MiG-19S's armament usually consisted of three Nudel'man-Rikhter lightweight NR-30 30mm cannon, with a single weapon mounted in each of the wing roots to avoid engine surge problems and a third in the nose. The wing root cannon had 70 rounds per gun and the weapon in the nose 55–70 rounds. All three cannon were belt-fed. Rate of fire was 850–1,000 rounds per minute, and the combined impact of the NR-30's 14.5-ounce projectiles was truly formidable. An ASP-5N optical gunsight and SRD-1M gun ranging radar provided aiming data.

The majority of the VPAF's 44 MiG-19Ss, supplied in 1968–69, were Shenyang-built. However, these aircraft may have been supplemented by a small number of Soviet examples in 1969.

F-4J PHANTOM II AND MiG-17F COMPARISON SPECIFICATIONS

	F-4J-28-MC Phantom II	MiG-17F
Powerplant	two GE J-79-GE-10, each rated at 17,900lbs maximum thrust	one Klimov VK-1F rated at 7,452lbs in afterburner
Dimensions		
Wingspan	38ft 4in.	31ft 7in.
Length	58ft 3in.	36ft 5in.
Height	16ft 6in.	12ft 5in.
Wing area	530 sq. ft	243 sq. ft
Weights		
Empty	30,778lb	8,664lb
Loaded (air combat)	56,000lb	13,858lb
Performance		
Max speed	1,428mph at 40,000ft	655mph at 38,000ft
Range	1,275 miles (with two external tanks)	646 miles (with two external tanks)
Climb	41,250ft per minute	12,795ft per minute
Service ceiling	54,700ft	48,446ft
Armament: (air-to-air)	4 x AIM-7E Sparrow III 4 x AIM-9G Sidewinder	1 x N-37 37mm cannon 2 x NR-23 23mm cannon

The MiG-19's massive single wing-fences, each 1ft 0.6in. tall, replaced three on each MiG-17 wing. As with earlier MiGs, the "Farmer's" rear fuselage could be detached for engine access. An unpainted MiG-19S was sometimes used as bait for US fighters, which would in turn be jumped by camouflaged MiG-17s in "pop-up" attacks from low altitude. This particular aircraft is a Chinese-built J-6, and it has been on display in the VPAF Museum in Hanoi for many years. (Dr István Toperczer)

THE STRATEGIC SITUATION

The first batch of Soviet-built VPAF MiG-17s was flown in from China to Noi Bai on August 6, 1964. Aircraft 2014 was reportedly piloted by 1Lt Pham Ngoc Lan, who was the second to land on that first delivery flight. Tran Hanh subsequently used this "Fresco" during the MiG-17's first combat engagement on April 3, 1965, when fellow 921st FR pilot Pham Ngoc Lan reported, "When in range I opened fire with my cannon and the F-8 Crusader in front of me exploded in a ball of fire. I was later credited with the first American fighter-bomber to be shot down by a VPAF pilot". In fact, VF-211's Lt Cdr Spence Thomas managed to limp back to Da Nang with his badly damaged F-8E. Four VF-151 Phantom IIs were flying as the Crusader's TARCAP that day, but they failed to engage the MiGs. (via Dr István Toperczer)

Shortly after World War II had ended, 27 planned aircraft carriers for the US Navy were cancelled and the job of providing America's nuclear deterrent was given to Strategic Air Command, formed in March 1946. It was equipped with long-range multi-engined bombers that could carry nuclear weapons that were too large for contemporary naval attack aircraft. The promised supercarrier USS *United States* was cancelled in 1949, and when a nuclear role was finally found for the US Navy, weapons were to be delivered by missile-armed submarines. Temporarily, the aircraft carrier was not considered a primary means of global power projection.

The Korean War showed that long-range nuclear bombers were not appropriate for distant "local" conflicts, and the lack of air bases in the region hampered the rapid deployment of tactical aircraft. Aircraft carriers were once again regarded as an ideal means of delivering tactical air strikes at short notice from secure seaborne "runways" virtually anywhere in the world. The US Navy commissioned the first of four 60,000-ton *Forrestal* class supercarriers in October 1955, augmenting 20 frontline "flattops".

Four *Kitty Hawk* class carriers and the one-off nuclear-powered USS *Enterprise* (CVAN-65) would follow in the 1960s.

The US Navy maintained a strong presence in Southeast Asian waters in the wake of the Korean War. As the defeated French withdrew from Dien Bien Phu in March 1954, three American carriers were close enough to provide support if required. When war in Southeast Asia recommenced in 1964, the Pacific Fleet had nine carriers assigned to it, each with full air wings of up to 90 aircraft. The new vessels had angled decks, an innovation also retro-fitted to three late-1940s *Midway*-class ships. Atlantic Fleet carriers were also drafted in as the war developed to ensure that there was no shortfall in naval air power in the region.

During the Gulf of Tonkin incident on August 2, 1964, when the destroyer USS *Maddox* (DD-731) was attacked by North Vietnamese gunboats that possibly mistook the vessel for a South Vietnamese warship, the US Navy's Pacific Fleet had three carrier air wings (CVWs) operating in the area. Only one had F-4B Phantom IIs aboard, however – CVW-14, embarked in USS *Constellation* (CV-64), included 24 F-4Bs of VF-142 and VF-143. The other two fighter-capable carriers were equipped with F-8E Crusaders.

Phantom IIs gradually replaced F-8s in the fighter squadrons on larger carriers, although at the time of the Tonkin Incident Crusaders outnumbered Phantom IIs (19 squadrons against 9 with F-4s) and eventually shot down 18 MiGs. In the first two war cruises for CVW-2 and CVW-15, each had one squadron of F-8Ds and one of F-4Bs. In these situations, the Crusader pilots still saw themselves as the "day-fighters", while F-4 crews handled "Fleet defence" or dropped bombs. Unlike Phantom II crews, the F-8 pilots were well trained in air-to-air combat. Gunnery, a redundant skill for F-4 pilots, was still practised with almost religious intensity in the Crusader community. However, on the first USS *Midway* (CVA-41) war cruise, the only MiG kills were claimed by F-4Bs of VF-21.

Following the *Maddox* attacks and President Lyndon B. Johnson's "limited and fitting response" in the form of Operation *Pierce Arrow* naval air strikes, the Pacific Fleet's Task Force 77 was reinforced by *Ranger*.

On August 6, 1964, the VPAF's 921st FR, led by Dao Dinh Luyen, began to fly its MiG-17s from the Chinese training base at Mong Tu to its new frontline home at Noi Bai, near Hanoi.

Thus the confrontation for the following seven years was established. Carriers operated from *Yankee Station*, at a safe distance from the North Vietnamese coast, but still close enough to allow air strikes to carry heavy bomb loads without having to air-refuel several times like USAF fighters flying from Thai bases. US Navy KA-3 Skywarrior tankers were normally only used for emergencies.

Cdr Lou Page, VF-21's executive officer, and Lt J. C. Smith pose with "Sundown 101" after claiming the first official MiG-17 kills on June 17, 1965. Page had more than 4,000 hours on fighters, and had also flown AD Skyraiders in the Korean War. Smith, also an ex-attack pilot, had made the switch to the rear seat of the Phantom II in 1959, and was fundamental in establishing procedures for F-4 RIOs at VF-121 and *Topgun*. He also helped change US Navy attitudes so that RIOs eventually had the same status as pilots. (US Navy)

Gen William C. Westmoreland, who was effectively running the war as field commander in-theatre, asked for a second carrier station, as he was so impressed with the US Navy's close air support in South Vietnam. *Dixie Station* was duly established to the south for this very purpose, and it also served as a "warm up" area for carriers that would eventually be moved north to *Yankee Station*.

By June 1965, with four carriers on station, Task Force 77 had fully evolved its wartime operations pattern. Vessels would usually spend seven months (often extended) on *Yankee Station*, split into 25+ "line periods", with "rest and recreation" port calls in Japan, Hong Kong or the Philippines in between. "Cyclic operations" required a 12-hour period (midnight to midday, or midday to midnight) of launching and recovering strikes every 90 minutes, followed by 12 hours in which to replenish stores and plan the next operational cycle while another carrier launched strikes.

During a 12-hour period three strike groups, each of up to 40 aircraft, could be despatched from a carrier track as little as 20 miles offshore. Larger attacks on major targets, usually in the Hanoi/Haiphong area, required the carrier's entire air wing for an Alpha strike. Cyclic ops could resume about two hours after an Alpha strike had returned.

The location from which the Task Force 77 carrier air wings attacked North Vietnam was known as *Yankee Station*. It was focused on a point at 16 degrees North and 110 degrees East some 100 miles offshore that had been the start point for the "Yankee Team" armed reconnaissance missions which preceded the war. A *Red Crown* warship 60 miles offshore provided radar coverage of the Red River valley for American strike aircraft, and in July 1966 a Positive Identification and Radar Advisory Zone (PIRAZ) was established with two other US Navy vessels to further extend radar coverage and MiG warnings. When on *Yankee Station*, three or four carriers would work in two adjacent operating areas, the northern circle extending 35 nautical miles from fixed point ZZ. In the northern ("blue") half of this circle, a carrier would alternate its air operations with another flattop in the southern ("gold") semicircle in 12-hour shifts. A second operating circle to the southeast was divided into "red" (north) and "grey" (south) operating areas, working in the same cycle. The southern *Dixie Station* was created on May 15, 1965.

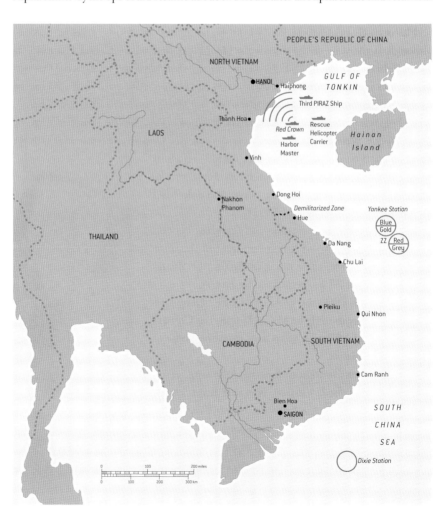

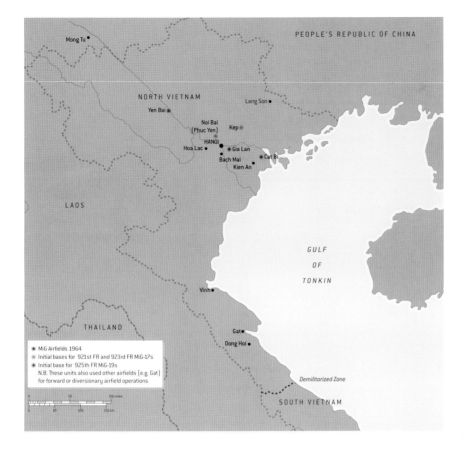

MiG Airfields 1964
Initial bases for 921st FR and 923rd FR MiG-17s
Initial base for 925th FR MiG-19s
N.B. These units also used other airfields (e.g. Gat)
for forward or diversionary airfield operations

Although the VPAF already had ten operational bases for its transport, training and radar units by 1963, it lacked fighter bases. Kien An, Gia Lam (Hanoi Airport), Cat Bi and other smaller fields were refurbished from 1955, and the first dedicated fighter base, Noi Bai, was begun with Chinese assistance in 1960 using a 10,000-strong workforce. An extensive maintenance base was also built at Bach Mai, in Hanoi, to assemble and repair aircraft – Mil Mi-6 helicopters from Gia Lam would transport damaged fighters in as underslung loads. By 1967 Hoa Lac, Tho Xuan and a modern base at Kep were available to defend the heart of the country. Small forward fields were added further south to attack B-52s and US Navy warships operating off the North Vietnamese coast.

F-4 squadrons usually provided four or six aircraft for a barrier combat air patrol (BARCAP) to protect a cyclic strike and two or four more for a target combat air patrol (TARCAP) or MiGCAP (usually at the rear of the formation) to intercept enemy fighters over the target area. More than 65 per cent of US Navy MiG kills were scored by TARCAP or MiGCAP fighters. This operational routine remained substantially unchanged throughout the war.

For MiG squadrons, their task was ostensibly much simpler. From relatively secure land bases, they would fly with comprehensive radar and GCI support to meet well-signalled incoming naval strikes, knock out as many bomb-laden attack aircraft as possible and return, after short missions, to their home bases or to emergency refuges in China if US fighters pursued them. In practice their task was much harder.

A shortage of pilots and aircraft, attacks on their bases after April 24, 1967 and primitive resources for maintenance and storage reduced their effectiveness. Working within the increasingly intensive network of AAA and SAM defences around North Vietnam's main target areas, MiG pilots had to rigidly obey GCI orders so as to avoid being shot down by their own defences, although some were nevertheless. GCI information came from an extensive, well-coordinated, early-warning radar network supplemented by visual "spotters" throughout the area and on Soviet spy-ships. The American radar and airborne coordination system was technically more complex, but it still could not always "see" MiGs at lower altitudes in order to warn its pilots. There

VF-114 "Aardvarks" was one of the earliest F-4B squadrons in the fleet, embarking with VF-213 in *Kitty Hawk* with CVW-11 for the vessel's October 1965-June 1966 Westpac cruise. It was a bitter initiation to the war in Vietnam for the air wing, which suffered 20 combat and five operational losses (including a KA-3B tanker to Chinese MiG-17s), and claimed no MiG kills in return. Pilot Lt "Fritz" Klumpp was one of CVW-11's Naval Aviators to fall victim to enemy fire, his jet being hit by AAA on his 30th VF-114 mission on January 31, 1966. "We made it to the water before being forced to eject. I was back in the cockpit two days later, and had completed 106 more missions by the end of May". The squadron's "Aardvark" logo was chosen by RIO Kirk Sheehan, as "its tongue could reach out a long way and zap ants, as the F-4 could do to its enemies". (via Norm Taylor)

were also frequent coordination problems between the various airborne, ship-based (*Red Crown*) or land intelligence agencies.

MiG-17 pilots soon realised that they could tackle US fighters at low and medium altitudes by luring them into turning fights, having first evaded their missiles by hard manoeuvring. Their numerical disadvantage was compensated by effective GCI, keeping them away from escorting enemy fighters, and by combining their efforts with R-3S "Atoll"-firing MiG-21s. The MiG-17 force also rapidly increased. By 1968, the two fighter regiments (the 921st and 923rd) had doubled in size from 36 to 72 pilots, and boosted their "Fresco-C" ranks from 35 jets in 1964 to more than 170.

At the end of 1965, to simplify the allocation of targets in the North, the US Navy and USAF divided North Vietnam into six "Route Packages" that extended from the demilitarised zone to the 25–30 mile wide buffer zone along the border with China. Naval squadrons were allocated Route Packs (RPs) II, III and IV in the central area of the country and the eastern section of RP VI (specifically VIB, which covered the area surrounding Haiphong harbour). For the USAF, this meant that the majority of its strike force, based in Thailand, had to cross through RP V or RP I to reach its most

lucrative targets in RP VIA – the Hanoi area. This duly increased its units' exposure to MiGs. USAF squadrons often flew near bases that were occupied by the numerically small, but deadly, MiG-21 force, while US Navy units more often encountered MiG-17s.

All potential targets required approval from the White House before they could be attacked, and many were struck over and over again at rather predictable times until the Pentagon considered them completely destroyed. This simplified the task of the defenders, who could predict the routes for naval strikes and follow them on radar from the moment they left the carrier. Radar sites, MiG maintenance depots and SAM sites were off-limits as targets for most of the war mainly because of the presence of Soviet "advisors".

President Lyndon B. Johnson's Operation *Rolling Thunder* policy of gradually advancing the "bombing line" towards Hanoi and Haiphong, hoping the North Vietnamese government would capitulate, gave the VPAF MiG-17 and MiG-19 pilots time to hone their skills, make good their losses and study US tactics. Diversionary airfields were built and aircraft were carefully hidden in "farm building" maintenance shelters near their bases. Others were parked in caves and transported to their bases by Russian helicopters. The rapid knock-out blows to airfields advocated by the Joint Chiefs of Staff in 1965 was met with the presidential response "Bomb, bomb, bomb. That's all you know!", but US pilots had to face the consequences of his hesitancy.

Although MiGs were never the most severe threat faced over the North (SAMs and AAA claimed far more US aircraft), their presence required huge defensive efforts on the part of carrier air wings. Rather than destroying MiGs on the ground or in transit from their suppliers, fighter crews were obliged to destroy them in the air, and then only when they threatened US forces. These rules of engagement changed little until President Richard Nixon's final onslaught in Operation *Linebacker II*, when the MiG force was effectively neutralised by unrestricted attacks on its airfields.

Lt Cdr John Nash flew with VF-213 on its first two combat cruises, and his squadron effectively wrote the F-4B's ground attack syllabus, based on the USAF "Dash-1" manual. Later, he developed it further with VF-121 and at *Topgun*. Flying captured MiGs in Project *Have Drill*, Nash helped evolve the following standard tactics for effective air combat against the MiG-17: "1. Never slow down with a MiG-17 in an F-4 or try to out-turn it. 2. Try to get a look-up shot with an AIM-7. 3. Use his restricted rearward visibility. 4. Take advantage of the MiG's inability to reverse his turn. The faster he goes the faster his roll rate decreases. At over 400 knots it is incredibly poor – less than 30 degrees per second". (Capt John Nash)

923rd FR pilots and their MiG-17s in 1972. Although their aircraft had remained substantially unchanged since 1964, the pilots replaced their World War II vintage SL-60 leather headgear with more modern added ZS-3 "hard" helmets. (Vietnamese Embassy Budapest via Dr István Toperczer)

THE COMBATANTS

In the early 1960s the US Navy quickly abandoned air-to-air combat training, preparing fighter aircrew almost entirely for air-to-ground warfare. It stuck to this policy right through to the end of Operation *Rolling Thunder* in October 1968. By then, however, the US Navy had conducted a detailed analysis of its air combat performance during this long-running campaign, emphasising the poor results its F-4 crews had obtained with AIM-7 and AIM-9 missiles, and amended its tactics accordingly. Its main conclusion was that Phantom II pilots were poorly prepared for air-to-air combat.

In selecting Naval Aviators to fly its new F-4B in 1961–65, the US Navy's training units had drawn on those with single-seat F4D Skyray, F8U Crusader or F3H Demon currency. Some had experience of radar-guided "lead collision" interception tactics using the Skyray's radar. Capt Tex Elliott, a member of the first operational F-4B squadron, VF-74, recalled, "The Skyray's radar scope gave you minimal flight information. On a low-altitude, in-the-rain, night attack against a NATO 'enemy', it occurred to me that I was doing two full-time jobs, and neither one as well as I wanted to. Therefore, I became a proponent of the two-seat interceptor".

Finding qualified back-seaters (originally called Naval Flight Officers, although McDonnell's term "Radar Intercept Officers" was preferred) to operate the Phantom II's far more sophisticated systems was difficult. Despite poor reliability, the AN/APQ-72 was superior to anything fitted in USAF interceptors, and it therefore required a highly-trained operator to get the best from it – although some pilots at first reckoned the RIO's cockpit wasted potential fuel space.

F-4B back-seaters boasted diverse backgrounds ranging from fighters to four-engined radar picket aircraft, and many were senior-ranking officers. Coordinating the two-man crew concept, rather than perpetuating a "master/servant" relationship as

VF-161 "Chargers" transitioned to F-4Bs in December 1964 and made the final US Navy Phantom II carrier launch (from *Midway*) in March 1986, having flown the F-4B, J, N and S variants. This F-4B, seen in the squadron's early markings, also had a long life. It first flew on October 11, 1963, and was eventually "expended" as a QF-4N target drone on September 25, 1990. VF-161 was paired with VF-151 from 1967 onwards, and it made three USS *Coral Sea* (CVA-43) Westpac deployments between August 1967 and July 1970. (US Navy via C. Moggeridge)

some established single-seat pilots preferred, took time. When the Naval Air Training and Operating Procedures Standardization (NATOPS) F-4 Flight Operations manual appeared, the responsibilities of both pilot and RIO were clearly set out, covering everything from flight planning to debriefing.

Suitable pilots were selected for full fighter courses early on in the syllabus, and the US Navy did not adopt USAF-style "quick conversion" courses for ex-transport or bomber crews so as to hastily fill gaps, although this in turn put pressure on crew numbers as the war escalated.

Viewing each mission as a two-man operation was certainly crucial to successful combat in Vietnam. The US Navy's only ace F-4 crew, Lt Randall "Duke" Cunningham and Lt(jg) Willy "Irish" Driscoll of VF-96, were good examples. Cunningham fully acknowledged that his sharp-eyed RIO enabled him to avoid or engage MiG-17s. Near the target, RIOs would often ignore their radar and concentrate on providing a second pair of eyes to monitor the threats.

The early squadrons also established operational routines for carrier operations, including optimum external fuel configurations. Capt "Hap" Chandler explained that, "Three tanks were dismissed right away. Two tanks restricted Mach and one tank restricted engine access, but had the least effect on speed. We ended up with one centreline tank, as the J79 was so gripe-free we didn't have to get to the engines hardly at all".

Pilots also learned to cope with the Phantom II's "nose heavy" take-off and landing characteristics, requiring the control column to be held rigidly fully aft on launch.

F-4 crews coming from basic training at Pensacola (where they usually flew TF-9J Cougars) for conversion training with VF-101 or VF-121 worked at interception techniques early on in their NATOPS syllabus. This section of the course saw pilots and NFOs perform eight sessions in the simulator followed by two familiarisation flights and ten more interception sorties, when they fired missiles at AQM-34 drones. This phase was followed by extensive ground-attack indoctrination and then 100 more sorties to develop interception skills against high-flying beyond visual range (BVR) targets, as well as cross-country navigation and general airmanship.

Any air-to-air practice was against other F-4s, making radar BVR interceptions on each other from 50 mile-range start points. Instructor Mike Shaw observed that, "F-4B pilots tended to be trained like airline captains, rather than combat pilots. We did very little air combat manoeuvring (ACM), and I suspect that many pilots went to Vietnam without ever having turned their Phantom IIs upside down!"

From 1966, initiatives within test and evaluation squadron VX-4 and the F-4 training units had led to a greater emphasis being placed on air-to-air training. In February 1969 Project *Have Drill* began operational testing of a captured MiG-17F by USAF and US Navy pilots, the latter led by Cdr "Tooter" Teague. This gave the Naval Aviators a much better understanding of the aircraft, and revealed weaknesses that could be exploited in combat – notably its uncontrollable tendency to enter a roll at 570 knots because the left wing warped. Those pilots that got to fly the "Fresco-C" also quickly realised that its flight controls were impossibly heavy ("locked in cement") above 525 knots at low altitude.

During the course of 255 *Have Drill* flights the MiG-17 was found to be simple, utterly reliable and strong. And although it could easily out-turn US fighters at low speeds, the communist jet was inferior to the F-4 in roll rate, acceleration, climb and overall controllability. The Phantom II's far greater power also gave it instant acceleration to separate from a MiG-17, rather than lose to it in a turning fight.

These revelations, and relevant combat tactics aimed at exploiting the "Fresco-C's" weaknesses, were incorporated in the so-called *Topgun* syllabus that was taught at the US Navy Fighter Weapons School (NFWS) after it was formally established on July 1, 1969, at NAS Miramar. The unit drew heavily on the core of personnel, research and experience in *Have Drill*, VF-121 and VX-4 in order to perform its mission. NFWS's aim was to disseminate effective air combat tactics throughout the fleet, and to place at least one *Topgun*-trained crew in each frontline squadron.

Brand-new F-4J BuNo 153790 in May 1967. VF-121 "Pacemakers" trained US Navy Phantom II crews at Miramar from December 1960 until September 1980, the unit receiving the first West Coast F-4J – a variant that it flew for 13 years. VF-121 and VX-4 were responsible for many of the innovations that transformed the US Navy's use of the Phantom II as a fighter. (Warren Bodie via Norm Taylor)

Garry Weigand (left) and Bill Freckleton (right) at the dedication of their MiG-killing (on March 6, 1972) F-4B "Old Nick 201" at NAS Key West in March 2008. Born in Scotland, Cdr Freckleton was commissioned in 1968 and trained at NAS Miramar as a RIO throughout 1970. He transitioned with VF-111 from the F-8 to the F-4B, embarking with the unit in *Coral Sea* in November 1971. Post-war he flew the F-4N and F-14A with the US Navy Reserve, instructed Iranian F-14 aircrew while with Grumman Aerospace and worked for Northrop Grumman, Boeing, Hughes Aircraft and Ford Aerospace, before acting as Range Control Officer for the F-22 Raptor Combined Test Force at Edwards AFB for nine years. In 2500 fighter hours he flew 117 combat missions and was awarded the Silver Star, Single Mission Air Medal, eight Strike/Flight Air Medals and the Navy Commendation Medal with Combat "V". (via Cdr Bill Freckleton Jr)

1969 also saw a review team headed by Capt Frank Ault deliver its thoroughly researched report on the design, manufacture and usage of the US Navy's air-to-air missiles. This document highlighted the many failures and problems experienced with the weapons, and suggested practical improvements.

Both of these initiatives would have a profound effect on the fleet's MiG encounters in the last year of the war.

For VPAF pilots, a very different situation prevailed. When they arrived at Noi Bai on August 6, 1964, they had been training on the MiG-17 for up to four years.

VPAF trainee Dang Ngoc Ngu, who survived combat until July 1972, is shown the cockpit of a MiG-17 by his Russian instructor, A. M. Yuriev, whilst in the Soviet Union. Students from more than 25 Communist countries undertook MiG training at the huge Krasnodar base complex throughout the 1960s and into the early 1970s. (via Dr István Toperczer)

FOSTER SCHULER "TOOTER" TEAGUE

Born in Louisiana in 1934, Foster Teague learned to fly at 13, and on graduation from Bossier High School in 1952 he entered Texas A&M University, where a promising football career was curtailed by a neck injury. On graduation in 1956, Teague began flight training, earning his Wings of Gold in 1958 and demonstrating the natural ability and supreme self-confidence that immediately directed him into a fighter squadron. Having initially flown the F11F-1 Tiger, he joined VF-211, which began his long-term devotion to the single-seat F-8 Crusader.

"Tooter", a nickname deriving from a childhood mispronunciation of his middle name, made four Vietnam combat cruises, flying 423 combat missions. On a second deployment with F-8E-equipped VF-111 "Sundowners" aboard USS *Oriskany* (CVA-34) in 1966, he became squadron Operations Officer. During the cruise, on August 31, he was flying as the solo escort for a reconnaissance mission being performed by VFP-63 Detachment G CO, Lt Cdr Tom Tucker. The latter was downed by AAA over Haiphong harbour, and Teague strafed North Vietnamese boats that were about to capture him. His determined defence of the downed Naval Aviator allowed a Sea King from HS-6 to make a successful rescue, and earned Teague his first Silver Star. A US Navy Commendation medal was awarded to him after a similar RESCAP effort for VF-162 F-8 pilot Lt(jg) R. F. Adams, who had been downed by AAA on 12 July 1966.

Finally, in the fire that devastated *Oriskany* on 26 October 1966, costing his CVW-16 25 pilots (44 officers and men were killed in total), Teague guided ten shipmates through smoke and darkness to safety.

VF-111 embarked Detachment 11 in USS *Intrepid* (CVS-11) from May to December 1967, with 'Tooter' in charge. During this time he bent Pentagon rules by destroying a MiG-17 parked on Noi Bai airfield and was shot down by AAA south of Haiphong on 12 August. Bailing out of his F-8C just offshore, he and the rescue parajumper were pulled three miles out to sea by a rescue helicopter so as to avoid intense ground fire, before being winched aboard.

Teague's next assignment saw him drafted into air test development squadron VX-4 following his suggestions for tactics against the MiG-17. In a year's assignment as US Navy team leader on the top-secret Project *Have Drill*, Teague extensively flew a captured MiG-17, exploring its

characteristics and evolving ways to fight it. His team took more than 120 US Navy pilots through combat sorties with the MiG, and visited every US Navy fighter unit to lecture on MiG-fighting tactics. Their work had a considerable impact on US fighter squadrons' results in aerial combat in 1972.

Returning to action in 1971, Teague assumed command of F-4B squadron VF-51 from Cdr Tom Tucker. This unit included several other experienced Crusader pilots within its ranks, namely Lt Cdrs Jerry Houston and Chuck Schroeder and Cdr Jack Finley. As an avowed single-seat exponent, "Tooter" took time adapting to the two-seat concept, but by mid-1972 he acknowledged that in VF-51's five successful MiG encounters all the "bandits" had been sighted first by back-seaters – so had four other MiG threats. His own MiG kill on June 11, 1972 (after damaging another in a March 1972 fight) exemplified this teamwork, and it made VF-51 an ace squadron – the photograph above shows Teague shortly after his MiG killing mission with the CO of CVA-63, Capt Bill Harris.

"Tooter" had five US Navy commands in all, including CVW-11, the fleet oiler USS *Kawishiwi* (AO-146) and the supercarrier USS *Kitty Hawk* (CV-63). He also served as Chief of Staff for Operations for the Seventh Fleet and Director of Current Operations and Crisis Management, Commander US Pacific Forces. He was awarded two Silver Star medals, six Distinguished Flying Crosses, a Bronze Star medal (V), the Legion of Merit, 14 Air Medals, five Navy Commendation medals and the Purple Heart. He died on August 29, 1998.

The first trainees had been in China and Russia since March 1956. Fifty aspiring fighter pilots in China, commanded by Pham Dung, were supported in North Vietnam from 1956 onwards by the First Flying School at Cat Bi and the Second Flying School at Gia Lam. Others were trained in Czechoslovakia as Ho Chi Minh's dream of an air force took shape. His recruits made up in enthusiasm for their deficiencies in basic technical education or physical fitness. Most came from far poorer backgrounds than their American counterparts, and all had to be taught basic Russian so as to be able to understand both the aircraft manuals and their instructors. Their political motivation was invariably strong, but it was constantly tested by their mentors, who regarded unswerving devotion to their patriotic cause as equal in importance to aptitude as a pilot. Often, more than three-quarters of students failed to complete the flight-training courses and were relegated to ground duties.

A shortage of aircraft and the lack of a suitable airfield in Vietnam meant that the first group of pilots remained in China after "graduating" on the MiG-17, flying MiG-15s instead. Generally, the Vietnamese students felt more at home with Chinese tutors, and had fewer communications problems than those being trained in Russia, despite the presence of translators. MiG-17s were soon provided for them at Son Dong, where the VPAF's first groundcrew were being instructed. In 1963 the entire operation was moved to Mong Tu, close to the North Vietnamese border. This base shift coincided with the arrival of 36 Soviet-supplied MiG-17Fs.

Three years earlier, on May 1, 1960, construction of Noi Bai airfield had begun, and the base was ready for the VPAF's single squadron, the 921st "Sao Do" (Red Star) Fighter Regiment, when it was led in by Dao Dinh Luyen on August 6, 1964.

Before venturing into combat, 921st FR pilots continued intensive training with increased flying hours in their MiG-17 "silver swallows" and MiG-15UTI trainers, supported by long sessions in primitive simulator cockpits. Aware that their fighters were inferior in numbers and technology to the Americans' equipment, they worked with their Soviet and Chinese advisors for another four months on tactics to integrate the obsolescent MiG-17 into North Vietnam's rapidly-developing network of anti-aircraft artillery (AAA) and radar. Like American pilots, they studied the tactics of World War II aces and worked on the assumption that "whoever fires first, wins".

Selection of suitable pilots for the first combat-ready sections of the 921st was a rigorous process. Some of the more over-enthusiastic individuals, including a few who favoured "kamikaze" ramming tactics, were restrained within the rigid doctrines of GCI taught by Soviet instructors. Some Vietnamese controllers, including Le Thanh Chon, were ex-MiG-17 pilots. In action, pilots became accustomed to sleeping under their jets when on alert duty, and "scrambling" before 0800 hrs.

When American air attacks began in earnest in 1965, the VPAF studied the predictable routes that the

The VPAF's first wing commander, Dao Dinh Luyen, was involved in training VPAF pilots from 1956 onwards. He was made CO of the 921st FR on its formation, and led the unit to Noi Bai from China in February 1964. In 1977 Dinh Luyen took command of the whole VPAF. (Tran Dinh Kiem via Dr István Toperczer)

restrictive rules of engagement forced the US Navy and USAF to follow to their targets. Interception tracks were duly planned to minimise exposure to enemy fighters and to take advantage of proximity to home territory and defences. Essentially, the pilots soon realised that they would have to orbit as "point defence" fighters close to likely targets, climbing from low altitude to hit the intruders. New bases were planned to place the short-range MiGs close to strategic targets. Above all, the country's radar network was extended to give sufficient warning of attack, particularly from the seaward side.

Flying was often limited by the Vietnamese climate, but this had been the same in the USSR, where the weather confined flying training to the summer. US Navy Phantom II trainees were used to the fine conditions that allowed all-year flying to take place in California, Florida and Virginia. In Russia, dogfighting training had been quite limited, and the VPAF pilots' small stature and light weight (sometimes below the minimum for safe use of the ejection seat) became a real handicap as they wrestled with the heavy controls of the MiG-17.

Basic training was initially performed on the piston-engined Yak-18 and, after 1966, on Czech-built L-29 Delfin jets, with 80 hours on this type followed by 40 hours on the MiG-17 at Kushchovsaya air base. A few L-29s were passed on to the VPAF in 1971.

The MiG-17 was considered obsolescent in Russia by mid-1957, used only for ground attack (for which it was not really suited) or training. The perceived wisdom on the MiG-17 versus other jet fighters was limited to the assessment of Chinese J-5s in evenly-matched combat with Taiwanese F-86Fs in 1960, or Egyptian and Syrian examples fighting Israeli Mystere IVAs in 1956 and 1960. Nothing was known about the aircraft's chances against more advanced American types. VPAF pilots had to establish those rules for themselves. Pham Ngoc Lan, senior pilot in the 921st FR in the spring of 1965, is credited with working out attack patterns that gave his squadron its first success against US Navy F-8s in April of that year. His training in China had lasted six years.

Another 30 pilots returned during the summer of 1965 from courses at Krasnodar Flight Officers' School on the Black Sea coast, where pilots from all corners of the Communist bloc were trained at a four-airfield complex. These men formed the nucleus of the second MiG-17 unit, the 923rd "Yen The" Fighter Regiment. At the same time the 921st FR began to induct its first MiG-21 pilots. Flying the "Fishbed" was the ambition of most MiG-17 pilots, but there were few examples available until later in the war.

Following the arrival of 18 more Krasnodar-trained pilots in November 1966, the VPAF's own 910th "Julius Fucik" Training Regiment began to produce aircrew. The first 14 were ready for action in January 1968, and all would be needed. By war's end North Vietnamese records listed 168 pilots killed in action – a large number for such a small country.

Pilot numbers early in 1964 (34 in total) were less than the numbers of available aircraft, but the training programme managed to generate more than three pilots for each MiG by 1970, despite a persistent lack of trainer aircraft.

Red-tailed MiG-17F 2533 takes off from Gia Lam in 1968. Once US strike aircraft started regularly targeting their airfields, the MiG units often sought the security of Gia Lam airfield in Hanoi. (via Peter Mersky)

The acquisition of MiG-19s caused the formation of a third squadron, the 925th FR, in February 1969 at Yen Bai. It flew both MiG-17s and MiG-19s, drawing pilots from Soviet MiG-21 courses and from the home-based 910th Training Regiment.

Fighter regiment had two or three squadrons on strength, each with at least eight fighters, commanded by a captain or lieutenant. Squadrons were in turn divided into flights, and pilots learned to operate as two pairs, or as a three-aircraft interception flight with a "lone wolf" killer MiG-17 some distance behind the leading pair.

Pham Hung Son (one of three similarly named pilots dubbed "Son A", "Son B" and "Son C") checks the 30mm cannon on his MiG-19S. He claimed three F-4 Phantom IIs destroyed, although his May 10 claim is the only verified success. As part of a four-aircraft interception flight with Cao Son Khao on his wing, Pham Hung Son was involved in a fight with F-4Ds from the 432nd TRW that saw triple MiG killers Maj Bob Lodge and Capt Roger Locher shot down (probably by Nguyen Manh Tung). Pham Hung Son also destroyed the 58th TFS F-4E flown by Capts J. L. Harris and D. E. Wilkinson. Although two pilots, Nguyen Manh Tung and Nguyen Hong Son, were killed in the action, it proved to be the MiG-19's best day in combat with the VPAF. (VPAF Museum via Dr István Toperczer)

NGUYEN VAN BAY

Of the 16 VPAF pilots credited with achieving ace status (five kills) in the Vietnam War, only three spent most of their time flying the MiG-17F. The most successful of these was Nguyen Van Bay.

Born in 1937 near Saigon, he moved to the North in 1952 to help in the resistance against French troops occupying his country, and remained there after the cease-fire. Van Bay signed up for air force training in 1962, and he was among the first to receive 200 hours/four years jet training in China, completing his course despite persistent air sickness.

Most trainees' discussion focused on dealing with the formidable F-4 Phantom II in combat, and one of Van Bay's first air-to-air engagements with the 923rd FR saw him tackling an F-4B from VF-151 near Kep on October 6, 1965. His MiG-17F was severely damaged by an AIM-9D fired by Lt Cdr Dan Macintyre and Lt(jg) Allen Johnson, who claimed to have shot the fighter down.

Van Bay enjoyed better success when he next fought US Navy fighters on June 21, 1966. An RF-8A from VFP-63 Det L, piloted by Lt Leonard Eastman (whose demise was attributed to AAA by the US Navy), and an F-8E from the VF-211 RESCAP flight were both lost. The latter machine, flown by Lt Cdr Cole Black, had already been damaged by AAA when it was jumped by Van Bay's four MiG-17s and shot down. Following 923rd FR policy, all members of the flight were awarded full kills for Black's shoot-down.

With wingman Vo Van Manh, Van Bay met Crusaders again on September 5 and fired at an F-8E from VF-111 flown by USAF exchange pilot Capt Wilfred Keese, who ejected after being hit in the canopy from a distance of just 250ft – a typical Van Bay tactic. He preferred using tracers rather than the gunsight to aim his weapons.

Van Bay's flight claimed Capt Murphy Jones' F-105D on June 29, although the latter's jet had also been hit by 85mm AAA. He tangled with F-4Bs again on April 24, 1967 when he attacked a VF-114 TARCAP. Both US Navy jets faced eight 923rd FR MiG-17s, SAMs and heavy AAA. After attacking two CAP sections unsuccessfully, the MiGs formed a defensive "wheel" and the F-4Bs entered it, but they were unable to achieve enough separation to fire AIM-9Ds. The aircraft crewed by Lt Cdr Charles Southwick and Ens Jim Laing met four MiG-17s head-on, and the Americans turned in behind them and destroyed one of their attackers with a Sidewinder. However, they were themselves downed by Van Bay moments later. Although the MiG pilots claimed four US aircraft that day, the only recorded casualty was the Southwick and Laing F-4B, which had already been damaged by AAA.

Van Bay met a US Navy strike the following day when he was one of four MiG-17 pilots forward-deployed to Kien An airfield. They intercepted four Skyhawks over a Haiphong target, and Lt Charles Stackhouse's A-4C was hit by MiG-17 gunfire, forcing the pilot to eject. Van Bay's flight received credit for this jet and Lt (jg) A. R. Crebo's A-4E (downed by a SAM according to US records).

Van Bay was decorated for his successes by Ho Chi Minh in 1967, and three years later he received a second medal from Cuban leader Gen Fidel Castro.

Still flying in 1971, Van Bay was one of ten pilots trained by a Cuban instructor to perform anti-shipping strikes from a forward airstrip at Gat using MiG-17s converted to carry 250kg bombs. They were to target US warships operating some 12 kilometres offshore on April 19, 1972. Wingman Le Xuan Di destroyed the 5-in. gun turret on the stern of USS *Higbee* (DD-806), while Van Bay flew southeast and slightly damaged the cruiser USS *Oklahoma City* (CLG-5). No BARCAP F-4s were encountered and both MiGs returned to base intact.

Van Bay retired from the VPAF in 1991 to farm his small-holding.

COMBAT

The US Navy Phantom II squadrons' first skirmishes with MiG-17s demonstrated both ends of the spectrum of success to confusion that characterised air combat during the 84 war cruises made by carrier-based F-4 units throughout the Vietnam War. As they were drawn into the conflict there was a dawning realisation in the F-4 training units that crews would be ill-prepared for air-to-air fighting. Capt Ken "Bullet" Baldry, an early member of VF-96, recalled, "As the fight in Vietnam warmed up, people in VF-121 'Pacemakers' (the West Coast F-4 training unit) became concerned that it was not going to be a war where you launched missiles at targets detected by radar over the horizon. You were going to have to go in and see who you were shooting at first, before firing off missiles. VF-96 was one of the first squadrons to give priority to ACM as a result of this stark realisation".

The outcome of VF-96's (and the F-4B's) first MiG engagement remains uncertain. Lt(jg) Terry Murphy and "rookie" Ens Ron Fegan were section leaders for a VF-96 BARCAP on April 9, 1965, replacing an F-4B that had crashed shortly after being launched from *Ranger*. The rapidly rearranged CAP entered its orbit as two separated sections, each on different radio frequencies. Murphy and Fegan, in "Showtime 611" (BuNo 151403), took their section close enough to Communist Chinese Hainan Island for four Chinese navy Shenyang F-5s from the Nanhai Naval Air Group to be launched from Lingshui Naval Air Force Base.

Turning to investigate the contacts on their radar scopes, Murphy and Fegan became separated from their wingmen, Lt Howie Watkins and Lt(jg) Jack Mueller, who in turn were attacked by a MiG-17F. The latter disengaged its afterburner and turned back for a second run at the F-4. Moments later Murphy apparently fired an AIM-7 at a MiG during a vertical manoeuvre, but he was not contactable again until an aircraft (possibly mistakenly identified as a MiG by Mueller) was seen falling away into the clouds in flames. Meanwhile, all three of the remaining VF-96 F-4Bs became involved in individual dogfights, and at least four AIM-7 and three AIM-9 launches were attempted, although all missiles either failed to track or did not leave the aircraft.

According to the pilot of the No 4 MiG-17F, Capt Li Dayun (interviewed in 1994 by a Joint Task Force investigator), "Showtime 611" was hit by one of these malfunctioning missiles and crashed just offshore, killing its crew. He reported that the four MiG pilots never received permission to fire, and claimed that all returned to base, although Murphy's crew was subsequently awarded a MiG kill.

The engagement was then "buried" so as to avoid provoking an international incident, but some problems that would arise over and over again in future combats were revealed for the first time. Poor communications, lack of flight formation integrity, unreliable missiles and out-of-parameters missile launches were to be frequent themes for the next seven years, as was the determination of the Chinese to defend their airspace. There were also other cases where Phantom IIs were accidentally fired on by "friendly" missiles.

Failed missiles (caused by attempting to launch an AIM-7 with the radar in "standby" mode) prevented VF-21 F-4Bs from making their first MiG-17 kill on June 4, 1965, but their next engagement was a textbook demonstration of Sparrow usage.

The unit's executive officer (XO), Cdr Lou Page, led a six-jet BARCAP from USS *Midway* (CVA-41) on June 17, with his expert RIO Lt J. C. Smith in the rear seat. Their wingman F-4B, "Sundown 102", was flown by Lt Dave Batson and RIO Lt Cdr Bob Doremus. Supporting a strike against the Ham Rong bridge, the jets patrolled at 12,000ft hoping to pick up some "bogies" on radar, and both Smith and Doremus got contacts at 45 miles north on their last "sweep" – MiGs attempting to catch the strike force with a rear attack as it departed. Following standard procedure, Smith took control and flew ahead to provide visual ID, which he assumed was required so that Batson, following at Sparrow-launching distance, could shoot at the target.

As Dave "Batman" Batson remembered, "We accelerated to 500 knots for better manoeuvrability. Lou was to set up a head-on attack, having made a positive ID. J. C. Smith took the farther target, creating a slight off-set to the head-on attack. This caused the MiGs to turn into the lead F-4. When they banked, their very distinctive wing plan

F-4B BuNo 152219 was flown by Lt David Batson and Lt Cdr Rob Doremus on the first official MiG-killing mission when the VF-21 crew shot down a MiG-17, probably flown by 1Lt Le Trong Long. Lt Batson recovered to *Midway* with "just enough fuel to land. I was showing 400lbs (about three minutes) at the top of the glideslope. After landing I taxied past our CO, Cdr Bill Franke, who was jumping up and down with his hands over his head. After shut-down, Rob came up from the back seat shook my hand and said, "Four more to go!"" (US Navy via C. Moggeridge)

1Lt Le Trong Long claimed to have shot down one of the F-4Bs involved in the June 17, 1965 engagement, although other VPAF sources indicate that he was actually the pilot who was shot down by the VF-21 crews that day. (via Dr István Toperczer)

was visible. Lou fired at close to minimum range while shouting 'It's MiGs!' I saw his missile fire, guide towards the formation and the warhead detonate. At first I thought it had missed, but then the outer half of the right wing came completely off the MiG and it started rolling out of control.

"I then put my full attention to the steering information on my radar scope, and I fired at minimum range. The AIM-7 shot off the rail on the right wing and swerved under the nose of the aeroplane. I lost sight of the missile but Rob saw it guide to a direct hit."

Page soon realised that each of the two contacts was actually a pair of close-flying MiGs, and his missile damaged the second jet in the trailing pair, which was the only one to return to base. Debris from Batson's kill also hit its wingman, and this MiG was belatedly (in 1997) awarded as a second kill for him. The VPAF counted just a single pilot, 1Lt Le Trong Long, as a loss on that day after his MiG crashed into a mountain. Phantom IIs from *Midway* had made the first official US Navy MiG kills of the war (its F-4 squadrons would claim eight victories by war's end), and on January 12, 1973 a VF-161 jet flown by Lt Vic Kovaleski and Lt(jg) Jim Wise would down a MiG-17 as the last US aerial victory of the conflict.

Returning to June 17, 1965, this engagement was an excellent example of the head-on AIM-7 interception for which the F-4B was built. Both crews avoided a close, turning fight with MiG-17s, and they withdrew as soon as their missiles had struck. There were to be few such engagements in coming years that followed these rules so closely.

The inexperienced MiG-17 pilots had clearly been taken by surprise by the VF-21 jets. Their rigid GCI guidance improved rapidly under Soviet supervision, and controllers soon learned to place their fighters where they would have an advantage over the Phantom IIs, preventing them from using their long-range missiles.

By July 10, 1965, the 921st FR had lost five MiG-17Fs and claimed just two USAF Phantom IIs in return. Non-combat related attrition had also been high. The unit was effectively stood down for retraining, and this resulted in very few encounters between F-4 crews and their MiG opponents for the next 11 months. Airfields, particularly the newly built Kep base, were improved during this period, and the training emphasis began to shift towards the MiG-21 rather than the MiG-17. Nevertheless, "Fresco" numbers increased to around 70, including a handful of all-weather MiG-17PFs. New pilots were instructed to avoid the escorting CAP Phantom IIs and concentrate on attacking the more vulnerable bombers (primarily A-4 Skyhawks and F-15 Thunderchiefs), forcing them to jettison their war-loads.

Following a two-month lull, from September VPAF MiGs were back in the air. The primary north-south supply route from North Vietnam to the south, dubbed "Route 1" by the Americans, was attacked by US Navy strike aircraft between Lang Son and Hanoi on September 20. A flight of four MiG-17Fs from the 921st FR was scrambled from Noi Bai to meet the intruders, as Pham Ngoc Lan recalled. "I was the leader of the flight, accompanied by Nguyen Nhat Chieu (a future MiG-17/21 ace), Tran Van Tri and Nguyen Ngoc Do, and as we climbed we spotted the American aircraft flying

MiG-17F COCKPIT

1. ASP-4NM gunsight
2. Throttle
3. Push-to-talk radio control
4. Aileron trim control
5. Flap and airbrake levers
6. ARK-5 radio compass tuning panel
7. Emergency canopy jettison
8. Cartridge-fired ejection seat
9. Ejection handles (both sides of seat)
10. Rudder pedals
11. Extendable control column with gun, speedbrake and ordnance/tank jettison buttons
12. Ordnance control panel
13. Emergency landing gear control
14. Canopy lock (right)
15. Canopy lock (left)

16. Windscreen de-mist and ventilation
17. Main pneumatic air pressure gauge
18. Main hydraulic pressure gauge
19. Aileron trim switches
20. Map/document holder
21. Bullet-proof windshield (64mm/2.5 inches thick)
22. Side-light transparency (8mm/0.31 inches thick)
23. Canopy sealing hose, pressurised to 3 bars (42.8psi)
24. KUS-1200 airspeed indicator
25. VD-17 altimeter
26. RV-2 radio altimeter
27. AGI-1 artificial horizon
28. EUP-46 turn-and-bank indicator (electric)
29. MS-15 Mach meter

30. VAR-75 vertical speed indicator
31. Padded gunsight reticle adjusting knob
32. White stripe for positioning control column in spin recovery
33. Pneumatic brakes control "bicycle" lever
34. Electrical panel
35. Panels for fire detection, fuel control and engine ignition
36. KES 857 fuel gauge
37. Landing gear select indicator
38. Flare select switch
39. Brake pressure gauge
40. ARK-5 Automatic Direction-Finding (ADF) indicator
41. DGMK-3 gyro compass display

42. EMI-3P fuel and oil pressure/temperature indicators
43. TE-15 engine rpm indicator
44. TGZ-47 engine exhaust gas temperature gauge
45. EM-10M indicator
46. Gyro-compass "align to north" button
47. Pilot's oxygen indicator
48. Undercarriage control handle
49. Undercarriage position indicator
50. Flap switch
51. VA-340 volt/ampere indicator
52. Master electrical switch
53. Cockpit over-pressure indicator
54. Extra armament control panel (some aircraft)

over Yen Tu at 3000m. We were ordered to drop our wing tanks, accelerate and attack. We immediately turned right and attacked a flight of four US Navy F-4s.

"The Phantom II pilots had not noticed us until it was too late. Two F-4s pulled hard up while the other pair broke to starboard. Not intending to go into a vertical fight, we stayed with the turning Phantom IIs. One of them was attempting to disappear into a cloud, while his wingman dived for the ground. My wingman, Nguyen Nhat Chieu, was in an ideal position to follow the lead F-4, which started to turn left into the cloud.

"The Phantom II's predicable flightpath allowed my wingman to take a short cut and close in on him. Popping out of the cloud, the F-4 headed for the sea, with Nguyen Nhat Chieu on his tail – he opened fire when he was within 400m of the Navy jet. Trailing black smoke, the F-4 began a slow descent and tried to escape, only to receive another burst from the MiG's trio of guns. The Phantom II crashed into a mountain near Nha Ham, in Ha Bac Province. Our flight returned home safely."

There was no official US Navy Phantom II combat loss recorded on this date, however.

The next MiG kill came on October 6, 1965 for Lt Cdr Dan Macintyre and Lt(jg) Allen Johnson in VF-151's "Switch Box 107" when an AIM-7 operated almost as advertised. Although the target MiG-17 appeared to be mortally damaged, no loss was recorded by the VPAF. However, future ranking "Fresco" ace Nguyen Van Bay landed his MiG-17 with more than 80 holes in its skin that day. Denied a second kill attempt when frustrated by Van Bay's wingman, and by his own wingman Lt Cdr Tom Ewall's decision to charge through the enemy fighters before re-entering the fight

Green "snake" MiG-17Fs of the 923rd FR at Kep air base. The silver rectangle just behind the intake is an access panel located on both sides of the nose on Shenyang J-5s, but only on the left side of Soviet-built MiG-17Fs. It was absent from "Fresco-A" models. The forward-hinged panel above the nose gave access to the R-800 radio equipment. Most MiG-17Fs had the perforated nose-wheel hub seen here, though some had a solid wheel. (VNA via Dr István Toperczer)

and attempting to turn with a MiG-17, Macintyre broke off from his own intended victim and drove away Ewall's aggressor, who was fortunately a poor shot. By then Macintyre was just 50ft above the ground, which rendered his missiles useless in any case because they could not break out a target from background clutter when it was so close to the ground.

The traditional "attack-run-return to re-engage" tactic inherited from the Phantom II community's pre-war interceptor days was increasingly criticised for failing to yield enough MiG kills. F-8s were engaging MiG-17s more successfully, mainly with AIM-9s, and air combat-experienced pilots like VF-143's XO Cdr Townsend joined numerous ex-Crusader exponents in demanding more adventurous manoeuvring tactics for the F-4B, including fighting in the vertical plane to use the fighter's power more effectively. He also wanted better use of the "loose deuce" pair to provide mutual support.

VF-161 "Chargers" entered the MiG-killing arena when Phantom II combat resumed on July 13, 1966. F-4B "Rock River 216" was crewed by Lt Bill "Squeaky" McGuigan and Lt(jg) Bob Fowler, the former having studied air-to-air tactics with the US Navy's air test and development squadron VX-4 prior to joining VF-161 – he took every opportunity to practise ACM once in the fleet. The TARCAP mission that McGuigan and his RIO were flying on the 13th was an extra one, as he had actually finished his tour the previous day. MiGs were expected, however, and he was keen to pit his skills against the enemy. McGuigan's division duly encountered four "Frescos", and he made VF-161's only *Rolling Thunder* MiG kill when he destroyed a grey-brown jet. This claim was also the first to be made by a US Navy Phantom II with an AIM-9B Sidewinder.

During the combat, the MiG-17s reportedly fired unguided rockets at the F-4s – Naval Aviators recounted similar attacks on several occasions during the conflict.

The rest of the "MiG-slaying" for 1966 was done by F-8 squadrons, although the year ended with the destruction of two An-2 biplanes by F-4Bs from VF-114 and VF-213 using AIM-7 missiles for some rather expensive night-time kills – crews from VF-142 and VF-143 had claimed similar victories on June 14, 1966.

MiG activity had steadily increased as the year had progressed, helped by the combat debut of the 923rd FR in March. There were changes in tactics too, with the close fighting formations previously employed by the VPAF being replaced by a more flexible 5,000ft spacing that allowed pilots more freedom to concentrate on their targets, rather than on formation-keeping.

The more successful pilots like Pham Ngoc Lan advocated World War II tactics – closing to within 1,000ft of the target so as to concentrate the gunfire. Others like Nguyen Nhat Chieu preferred to fire from even closer range, beginning to open up with short bursts at 600ft and moving in to secure the kill. This was possible if a Phantom II could be "jumped" in a surprise attack, or had lost energy during close-in fighting or suffered AAA damage. Conversely, the advice to F-4 pilots was always to "stay fast" and keep out of the MiG's gun-range of about a mile.

If VPAF pilots saw US missiles launched at them (easily done in the AIM-7's case due to its massive Thiokol smoke plume), they could usually employ the MiG-17's "turn on a dime" performance to defeat them with a 3-4g turn into the missile's track

1. Indicator control assembly
2. Utility panel, oxygen/cabin air control
3. Cockpit lights controls
4. Emergency canopy release
5. Communication/navigation control panel
6. UHF channel selector
7. True airspeed indicator
8. Altimeter
9. Utility light
10. Remote attitude indicator
11. Utility panel
12. Digital display indicator
13. Command target altitude indicator
14. Disable panel
15. Threat display indicator
16. Strobe display scope

17. Airspeed and Mach indicator
18. Bearing-distance-heading indicator
19. Low fuel/canopy lock/radar cooling lights
20. Clock
21. Wing lock indicators
22. Equipment cooling reset button
23. Manual canopy unlock
24. Radar antenna hand controller (stowable)
25. Extra UHF/ECM control panel (F-4N)
26. Radar scope
27. IFF selector panel
28. Arm rest for radar hand control use (folded)

29. Low-Altitude Bombing System (LABS) timer
30. Vertical gyro cut-out switch
31. AC power system test
32. Bus test button
33. Circuit breaker panels
34. Radar beacon control panel
35. AN/APX-76 IFF controls
36. AN/ALQ-91 control indicator
37. Emergency oxygen control
38. Drag chute release
39. Radar set control panel (stowable)
40. Navigation computer panel

41. Auxiliary radar set control panel
42. Emergency harness release handle
43. Command selector valve handle
44. Circuit breaker panels
45. Airborne Missile Control System (AMCS) air data calculator
46. Checklist
47. AN/APQ-72 radar control unit stowing lever
48. Radar set panel stowing lever
49. Martin-Baker Mk H5 ejection seat

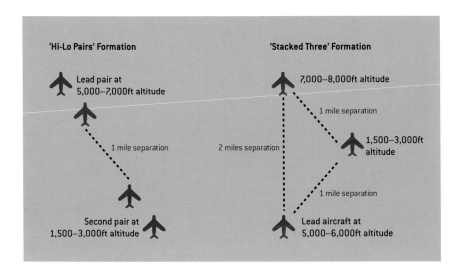

'Hi-Lo Pairs' Formation

Lead pair at 5,000–7,000ft altitude

1 mile separation

Second pair at 1,500–3,000ft altitude

'Stacked Three' Formation

7,000–8,000ft altitude

1 mile separation

2 miles separation

1,500–3,000ft altitude

1 mile separation

Lead aircraft at 5,000–6,000ft altitude

or a descending spiral manoeuvre. However, poor visibility from the MiG's cockpit often allowed an F-4 pilot to get into the blind area and shoot while the MiG was briefly in straight and level flight – the ideal circumstances which provided many of the confirmed kills.

During 1966 the MiG-17 units also worked on coordinated tactics with MiG-21s, and these were to prove effective throughout the war. A pair of MiG-21s attacked from high altitude, charging through the F-4 escorts at supersonic speed to make a slashing "Atoll" missile attack on the bombers, while MiG-17s caught them at a vulnerable point as they pulled up from a bombing run. As the strike force departed, more MiG-17s, scrambled on a signal provided by a bell made from an American bomb casing, approached from lower altitude to make "pop-up" rear attacks.

After USAF F-4s inflicted severe losses on the MiG-21 force in Operation *Bolo* on January 2, 1967, MiG activity declined and US Navy F-4 crews did not engage them again until April 24. During the lull in action, the MiG force increased in size to more than 110 aircraft, a new airfield was opened at Hoa Lac and a new Soviet-inspired tactic was introduced. The "wagon wheel" consisted of a circling group of six to eight MiG-17s whose pilots hoped to lure F-4s into the wheel so that they could use their superior rate of turn to get in behind them.

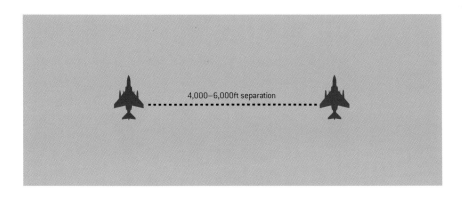

4,000–6,000ft separation

Although *Rolling Thunder* strikes increased from March onwards, the Pentagon still resisted the advice of the Commander-in-Chief Pacific Command, Adm U. S. Sharp, to attack strategic targets, including airfields. Secretary of Defense Robert S. McNamara did not regard MiGs as a serious enough threat to risk losses to the Russian advisors who were known to be working on VPAF bases. By April, increasing US aircraft losses to MiGs persuaded the Johnson administration to sanction limited airfield attacks on the 24th of that month. That day, VF-114 covered an attack on Kep in which Lt Cdr Charles Southwick and his RIO Ens Jim Laing and Lt Denny Wisely and RIO Lt(jg) Gary Anderson claimed two 923rd FR MiG-17s shot down. As previously mentioned, Southwick and Laing were then themselves downed by additional "Frescos". They spent the rest of the war as PoWs.

On August 10, VF-142 claimed the F-4B's first two MiG-21 kills, and three days later a lone Phantom II from the same unit encountered MiG-19s for the first time when it was attacked by six communist Chinese J-6s just south of the Chinese border. The crew evaded "Atoll" missiles and gunfire from them all. On September 21, two VF-161 F-4Bs repeatedly gained firing solutions on four MiG-17Fs but all six of their missiles failed to operate. They eventually had to fake a head-on attack on six "MiG-19s" that by then had joined the fight so as to make good their escape. Lt Dick Brent and Lt(jg) Miles Peinemann of VF-142 claimed a probable MiG-17 kill. Sister-squadron VF-143 got another MiG-21 on October 26.

MiG-17 losses continued throughout the remaining months of 1967, with ten being credited to F-8 Crusaders and one to VF-142 F-4B crew Lt Cdr "Geno" Lund and Lt(jg) "Bif" Borst on October 30, when they attacked Lt Tran Sam Ky's "Fresco". Lund recalled, "At 3-4 miles I already had it in range, and I got a 'tally-ho' (visual ID) on four MiG-17s in two sections – one which we were already locked on to and another

Nguyen Dinh Phuc (left) and Le Hai (right) were amongst seven pilots honoured by Ho Chi Minh in 1967 for their war efforts. Le Hai claimed six kills, including the VF-114 F-4B of Cdr Charles Southwick and Ens Jim Laing and, on November 19, 1967, another F-4B flown by Cdr Doug Clower and Lt(jg) Walt Estes. Nguyen Dinh Phuc claimed the second F-4B (of Lt(jg)s Jim Teague and Ted Stier) destroyed that day, but he was himself shot down by USAF F-105Fs one month later. (via Dr István Toperczer)

200–300ft astern. My AIM-7 guided absolutely perfectly and impacted the No 2 MiG. It hit just aft of the cockpit and he blew up and entered a flat spin".

Lund made a high yo-yo manoeuvre and headed for the second section, which he eventually worked his way behind for a second AIM-7 shot. "The AIM-7E left the launcher, and about 100ft from my aeroplane it exploded and broke up. I felt a jarring sensation in the jet. Apparently, the right engine had stalled and I didn't know it".

Damaged by missile debris, the engine was wrecked, but Lund continued to dogfight with the MiGs, just missing with an AIM-9 that he shot at a green jet. Eventually, the engine damage led to full hydraulic failure. Unable to refuel in-flight or lower their landing gear, the crew reluctantly ejected from "Dakota 203" five miles from USS *Constellation* (CVA-64).

MiG-17 pilots secured a degree of revenge on November 19 when they destroyed both F-4Bs from a VF-151 TARCAP (see cover art caption for a full description of this action). There is a possibility that one of the MiGs may have in turn been downed by a Sidewinder fired from the jet crewed by Lt Cdr Doug Clower and Lt(jg)Walt Estes prior to its demise.

During 1968–71, MiG-17 skirmishes were rare. Airfield attacks had driven most of the 80-strong force into its Chinese safe havens, and occasional clashes with MiG-21s brought three kills for US Navy crews flying the newly-acquired F-4J and a VF-92 F-4B loss to top MiG-21 ace Nguyen Van Coc. The "bombing halt" from November 1968 gave the VPAF time to repair its airfields and regroup its fighter units, which by 1972 could muster more than 130 MiG-17s and 30 MiG-19s. New initiatives were planned, including MiG-17 attacks on Seventh Fleet warships on April 19, 1972.

As the war heated up again in January 1972, leading to the North's spring invasion of South Vietnam, US Navy clashes with MiGs also resumed in quantity. The first success in 22 months went to VF-96's Lt Randall "Duke" Cunningham and Lt(jg) Willie Driscoll when they downed a MiG-21MF on January 19. Cunningham's previous RIO, Lt Lynn Batterman, noted that his pilot was utterly focused on MiG killing. "He worked harder than the average pilot and was better than average because of it. He and I were the only crew to consistently check out and re-read the secret manuals we had on MiGs (we even had some MiG repair/NATOPs manuals) that were controlled by the skipper, Cdr Al Newman".

Squadronmate Lt Matt Connelly, a double MiG-17 killer, recalled, "Between the 1970 and 1971–72 cruises, VF-96 undertook the *Topgun* academic syllabus. We flew tactics hops against *Topgun* jets, as well as other dissimilar aircraft, including USAF F-106s. During our turnaround missile shoot, VF-96 expended the entire West Coast training allowance for missiles. This did not make us popular with Westpac staff, but it later paid handsome dividends".

Following Cunningham's January kill, things went quiet again for almost two months until, on March 6, Lt Garry Weigand and Lt(jg) Bill Freckleton of VF-111 claimed the first MiG-17 destroyed by an US Navy Phantom II since November 1967. This particular success was a good example of the F-4's versatility. Limited maintenance provision and small aircraft numbers meant that Phantom IIs often had to be launched without fully operational systems. Bill Freckleton remembered, "It was not unusual in our air wing (CVW-15) to launch at least one aircraft in a section with a known, pre-launch radar discrepancy". Their F-4B "Old Nick 201" had no radar, and wingman Jim Stillinger's jet had a "search only" capability.

Instead, the Phantom II crews relied on the skill of *Red Crown* fighter controller Chief Radarman Larry Nowell on board USS *Chicago* (CG-11), which was sailing just off the North Vietnamese coast in the Gulf of Tonkin. Nowell, who was eventually credited with assisting in the destruction of 12 MiGs in 1972, guided the section of VF-111 jets to a point where they could visually ID the approaching MiG-17, whose well-trained pilot engaged Stillinger in a turning fight. He rolled out level, "dragging" the MiG behind him, which enabled Weigand and Freckleton to launch an AIM-9 into its afterburning tailpipe. Too low to bail out, Snr Lt Hoang Ioh was killed when his MiG hit a hillside and exploded. This two-on-one tactic was recommended by *Topgun* instructors.

May 1972 was a remarkable month for Seventh Fleet F-4 units, as they destroyed 11 MiG-17s, three MiG-21s and two MiG-19s in just 18 days of combat. VF-51's Lt Cdr Jerry Houston and RIO Lt(jg) Kevin Moore scored the first of three kills (the remaining two were MiG-21s claimed by VF-114) on May 6. A former F-8 expert, "Devil" Houston had flown *Have Drill* MiG-17s, and was therefore fully conversant with the jet's control problems at low altitude and high speed. With fellow senior flight leader Lt Cdr Chuck Schroeder, he heard strike leader (and *Topgun* pioneer) Lt Cdr Jim Ruliffson call out a MiG-17 that was closing on the tail of an A-6A Intruder flown by CVW-15 CO Cdr Roger Sheets. Both the US Navy bomber and the MiG were flying at low altitude down a karst valley. Accelerating to a position behind the "Fresco", Houston waited for the A-6 to break and give him an AIM-9 shot.

"CAG Sheets decided not to break until he saw that my missile had fired – the ultimate decoy", explained Houston. "It worked, but only because at the last minute

One of two MiG-17Fs modified for short-field landings and armed for anti-shipping attacks, this aircraft has resided in the VPAF Museum in Hanoi for many years. Russian PROSAB-250 bombs were hung on underwing pylons and a braking parachute was added in a bullet fairing at the base of the fin. Large numbers of torpedo boats set out to attack the *Higbee* after it was damaged by Le Xuan Di's MiG-17, but they were driven off by gunfire from the destroyer *Sterett*.
(Dr István Toperczer)

(approaching minimum firing range, and in total frustration) I decided to fire, despite there being a chance that the weapon could have been locked onto CAG's A-6. I didn't know that he couldn't hear my frantic calls to 'Break and get the hell out of there'!

"All he heard was the transmitted Sidewinder tone. Our ex-US Marine Corps F-4B was old, and had a history of radio problems. On this particular occasion the Sidewinder tone was also transmitted, effectively blocking out the rest of our transmission."

Fortunately, Sheets broke at the right moment, but the MiG pilot (probably Nguyen Van Bay the Younger) could not make his control-locked aircraft turn. The AIM-9 blew off its tail at an altitude of just 100ft and the "Fresco" crashed.

Cunningham and Driscoll's first MiG-17 victory followed 48 hours later. As his wingman Lt Brian Grant described it, the engagement was a "classic over-water CAP vectored onto an overland MiG target", except that the latter had set a trap which Grant detected in time to make "a course reversal that placed Randy Cunningham behind me in a position to down his second MiG, conveniently trapped at my 'six o'clock'".

As the MiG pilot opened fire on Grant's "Showtime 101", Cunningham fired an AIM-9G to distract it while RIO Driscoll monitored two MiG-17s that had reversed their course and started to fire shells at "Showtime 112". Having this time acquired a missile lock tone, Cunningham quickly loosed off a second AIM-9 that disintegrated the MiG. "It was as classic a 'mutual support' textbook fight as we had practised in training", recalled Brian Grant.

Nguyen Phi Hung was involved in the shooting down of two VF-151 F-4Bs on November 19, 1967, when four 923rd FR fighters, operating from the forward airfield at Kien An, successfully bounced the US Navy jets as they provided TARCAP for aircraft attacking targets near Haiphong. (VPAF Museum via Dr István Toperczer)

May 10 yielded 11 claims by US fighters, with seven of them being MiG-17 kills credited to US Navy Phantom IIs. Five VPAF pilots were lost. The first two fell to Lts Matt Connelly and Lt Tom Blonski (see cover art caption for full combat description). During the same Alpha strike, Cunningham and Driscoll, armed for flak suppression, ran into MiGs from three VPAF bases over the Hai Duong target. They were in search of revenge for an audacious MiG-21 kill achieved by VF-92's Lt Curt Dosé and Lt Cdr Jim McDevitt over Kep's main runway that morning.

Within a minute Cunningham's "Showtime 100" had downed an attacking MiG-17, having forced it to overshoot into his AIM-9 range. Minutes later he spotted four F-4s trapped in a "wagon wheel" with eight MiG-17s. As VF-96 XO Cdr Dwight Timm emerged from the "wheel" with three MiGs on his tail, Cunningham attempted to come to his rescue, but was in turn set upon by two MiG-19s from above and four more MiG-17s from behind. Manoeuvring violently to shake off his pursuers, Cunningham got Timm to sharply break away from the "Frescos" that were trailing him. This cleared the way for "Showtime 100" to down a second MiG-17 with another AIM-9 shot.

Cunningham's tail was protected by Lt Steve Shoemaker and Lt(jg) Keith Crenshaw, who saw another "Fresco" moving into a firing position behind "Showtime 100". They destroyed the VPAF jet with a single AIM-9. Yet another MiG-17 then began to fire cannon rounds at Cunningham in a head-on pass. The latter used his *Topgun* training to deal with the new threat, pulling the F-4 in a vertical climb in order to throw off the "Fresco" pilot's aim. Surprisingly, the MiG pilot followed suit, and two further vertical climb and rolling scissors manoeuvres left both fighters short of speed, but with the MiG behind the F-4J.

Lt Matt Connelly uses the universal pilots' "hand language" to run through his double MiG kill while RIO Lt Tom Blonski looks on thoughtfully. In Matt Connelly's opinion, "The F-4 was actually ill-suited to close-in dogfighting due to its limited g available below 420 knots and the lack of a Gatling gun. The MiG-17 and MiG-21 had one full g advantage below 420 knots. However, *Topgun* taught us how to fly the F-4 to its advantage and capitalise on the weaknesses of enemy aircraft".
(US Navy via R. F. Dorr)

Former *Blue Angels* pilot Lt Steven Shoemaker and Lt(jg) Keith Crenshaw pose with "Showtime 102", which displays all eight of VF-96's MiG kills. They contributed the last MiG to be downed on May 10, 1972 while flying BuNo 155749 "Showtime 111". (US Navy via Peter Mersky)

Resorting to desperate measures during the third climbing pursuit, Cunningham cut the throttles and briefly extended his airbrakes, throwing the MiG out in front of him. The VPAF pilot, probably at "bingo" fuel, sought to dive away towards Kep, but Cunningham managed to push the nose of his almost stalling F-4J over and fire an AIM-9 that caused enough damage for the MiG to crash into the ground and confer ace status on Cunningham and Driscoll. They were the first Americans to achieve this accolade in the Vietnam War, and the only Naval Aviators to do so, period.

Heading back out to the shore, Cunningham was pursued by yet another MiG-17, sitting close behind him and possibly firing his cannons. Matt Connelly swung over towards it, fired an unguided AIM-7 from his "radarless" F-4J and scared the MiG away. Two more MiG-17s and a MiG-21 sought to engage the harassed fighter as it neared the coast, but "Showtime 100's" fate was probably determined by a SAM explosion

65

"We believed in the Sidewinder. The radars weren't reliable and we feared that their strobes might have given away our presence and cost us a shot in a MiG engagement. The missile of choice was always the Sidewinder. Always! We would fly into a kill position for the Sidewinder, and once you did that a kill was practically assured."

Thus Jerry B. Houston, VF-51 MiG killer, expressed the feelings of most US Navy Phantom II pilots during the final years of the war.

The original F-4 concept saw the AIM-9 as a last-resort back-up for the main AIM-7 Sparrow armament. A potentially hostile "bogie" would be identified on radar in "search" mode by the RIO at up to 80+ miles. If intelligence sources confirmed it as a "bandit" ("red" bandits were MiG-17s, "white" were MiG-19s and "blue" were MiG-21s), the RIO used his hand controller to lock the AN/APQ-72 radar antenna onto the blip and both he and the pilot would see the range decrease as it moved down on a vertical line on their screens.

A small "pipper" appeared at the centre of a circle on the screen (repeated on the pilot's gunsight). This changed from white to red when the aircraft was inside launch parameters. If the pilot had selected "interlocks in" on his missile panel, an AIM-7 would then fire when the trigger was pressed. The aircraft then had to be pointed at the target for up to 25 seconds at typical range or the missile would lose guidance from the F-4's radar and "go ballistic".

While the AIM-7 could be useful in head-on attacks at long range, most pilots found themselves at closer range, where the Sidewinder excelled. The pilot had to approach his target from behind, use his "pipper" as for the AIM-7, select "heat" on his three-way missile selector switch and then listen for a "growl" in his headphones, which indicated that the missile's infrared seeker had acquired a heat source (preferably a MiG in afterburner). If no tone was received, he would cycle the switch to select another missile. Once released, the AIM-9 found its own way to the target.

near-miss that damaged its hydraulics. Fighting to maintain control of the failing systems by using afterburner and extreme rudder-induced rolls, the crew was finally forced to eject, and rely on HH-3A helicopters from HC-7 to return them to *Constellation*.

The seventh, and last, MiG-17 to fall victim to a Sidewinder that day was hit by a VF-51 F-4B flown by Lts Ken Cannon and Roy Morris in a one-on-one clash with a pilot that Jerry Houston described as a "damn tough and experienced opponent". The MiG was about to ease in behind Chuck Schroeder's F-4B when "Ragin' Cajun" Cannon caught up with it and fired.

On May 18 Lts Nick Criss and Ken Culverson of VF-213 probably downed yet another MiG-17, and two crews from VF-161 were credited with destroying the only MiG-19s to fall to the US Navy. These victories came when two MiG-19S "Farmers" of the 925th FR attempted to oppose a CVW-15 strike as it approached the regiment's base at Kep.

Topgun graduate Lt Henry "Bart" Bartholomay and his RIO Lt Oran Brown, in "Rock River 110", with Lts Pat Arwood and James "Taco" Bell in "Rock River 105" (who were on their very first mission over North Vietnam), were the MiGCAP for *Midway's* strike aircraft. Bartholomay picked up a distant sun glint from a shiny wing, and closer investigation revealed a pair of silver MiG-19s approaching Kep to land. Positioning Arwood at 3,000ft, he dived to pursue the MiGs. The "Farmer" pilots spotted the Phantom IIs and split up, with an F-4 following each VPAF interceptor through a series of 7g turns over Kep that caused the jets to rapidly bleed off energy.

"Bart" soon extended two miles away to rebuild his speed, while Oran Brown kept sight of the enemy. As he returned, the MiG pilot who was circling with Arwood decided to go for "Bart's" Phantom II instead, and thereby presented Arwood with an opportunity to fire two AIM-9s successfully at the "Farmer", which stalled and crashed.

Rather than re-enter a turning fight with the remaining MiG, "Bart" allowed it to get on his tail. As the MiG-19 approached firing range, he threw his Phantom II into an outside barrel roll, with flaps and speed-brakes extended and throttles cut to idle. This forced the MiG to overshoot and climb sharply. Regaining energy in afterburner, "Bart" followed him vertically up to 5,000ft until both aircraft were almost stalling.

As VF-51's "Screaming Eagle 111", this battered ex-Marine Corps F-4B provided Lts Ken Cannon and Roy Morris with their MiG-17 kill on May 10, 1972. It was actually assigned to Lts Winston Copeland and Dale Arends at the time. Ironically, Copeland and his RIO Lt Don Bouchoux used Cannon's assigned aircraft (BuNo 149457) for their own MiG-17 kill on June 11, 1972. (via Brad Elward)

Fresh from the heat of battle on May 18, 1972, Lts Oran Brown, "Bart" Bartholomay, Pat Arwood and Mike "Taco" Bell pose for a photograph in the VF-161 ready room aboard *Midway* after claiming the US Navy's only MiG-19 kills. As Bart recalled, at very low altitude "I pulled back into the MiG but couldn't hear a Sidewinder tone. I knew we were desperately low on fuel, so I made a decision to try one more time. This time I still couldn't hear an AIM-9 tone, but went ahead and fired. To this day I don't know whether he was hit by my missile or I just flew him into the ground". (US Navy)

As the two jets nosed over, the VF-161 pilot was able to edge in behind the MiG-19 until they both pulled out at an altitude of below 100ft. "Bart" fired an AIM-9 at minimum range and accelerated close to the MiG as its right wing suddenly dipped. The pilot instantly ejected and the aircraft crashed into the ground. Both VF-161 crews were awarded kills.

The unit chalked up a second double-kill when *Topgun* veteran Lt Cdr "Mugs" McKeown and Lt Jack Ensch, with Lt Mike Rabb and Lt(jg) Ken Crandall, mounted a MiGCAP for a May 23 Haiphong strike. Crandall's radar failed and Jack Ensch's could not detect the low-flying MiGs that they had been warned about by the *Red Crown* controller aboard USS *Biddle* (DLG-34).

Suddenly finding themselves on approach to Kep airfield, the VF-161 crews were alarmed to see two MiG-19s flash through their formation, followed by four MiG-17s to seal the trap. Rabb went into a turning fight with one pair at treetop altitude, while McKeown, in "Rock River 100", was set upon by two MiG-17s and the pair of MiG-19s. Pulling hard into one of the "Frescos", he employed a well-tried *Topgun* "last resort" trick and allowed his F-4B to "depart" out of control by "cross-controlling" its rudder and ailerons. McKeown recovered at 2,000ft, lost the pursuing MiG-17 and found another ahead of him. He turned into the latter jet's blind spot and destroyed it with an

Lt(jg) Ken Crandall, assigned RIO of this VF-161 Phantom II, was flying with Lt Mike Rabb on May 23, 1972 as wingman to Lt Cdr Ron "Mugs" McKeown and Lt Jack "Fingers" Ensch when they scored their two MiG-17 kills. "Bart" Bartholomay and "Taco" Bell took responsibility for the "Chargers'" squadron livery, which was an adaptation of the NFL San Diego Chargers' team colours. (R. Besecker via Norm Taylor)

AIM-9G. Rabb, meanwhile, had another MiG-17 on his tail that had fired at him unsuccessfully, and he "dragged" it out for McKeown to make his second AIM-9 kill.

VF-51 added two more MiG-17s to its score on June 11 – the final day of a line period for its carrier, USS *Coral Sea* (CVA-43). A MiGCAP element comprising Cdr "Tooter" Teague and Lt Ralph Howell, with Lts Winston Copeland and Don Bouchoux, was vectored onto four low-flying MiG-17s. Neither F-4B had a serviceable radar, and "Mad Dog" Copeland's jet had no radio either, but the MiGs were acquired visually from the CAP's 3,000ft altitude at a distance of three miles. As the F-4s turned in behind the formation, with Copeland climbing a little higher, the MiGs split. Copeland immediately shot down the leader, who had climbed to 800ft, and Teague stayed with a MiG that continued in straight and level flight, hitting it with the second AIM-9G he selected.

While it fell away in flames, he turned towards a MiG-17 that had banked away to the right and fired another AIM-9. The MiG pilot made a sharp turn and the missile exploded close to its tail, damaging the fighter. The "Screaming Eagles" then headed for the beach, with MiG-21s vectored onto them, but Copeland's jet was hit by ground-fire as it went "feet wet". He managed to make a single-engined carrier landing, but the Phantom II (BuNo 149457) was so badly damaged that it was eventually struck off.

On July 10 Lts Robert Randall and Frederick Masterson of VF-103 were shot down during a MiGCAP over Kep. Randall was dogfighting with a MiG-17 at the time when his aircraft was hit either by AAA or, more likely, cannon fire from a second 'Fresco'. The aft end of the F-4J erupted in flames and the crew ejected and were captured. The jet's demise was credited to Hanh Vinh Tuong of the 923rd FR, who the VPAF claimed was killed later in this engagement – no claims were made by American crews on this date, however. This VF-103 Phantom II was the only US Navy fighter credited to a MiG-17 in 1972–73.

The last US Navy MiG kill of the Vietnam War came on January 12, 1973, when VF-161's Lt Vic Kovaleski and Lt(jg) Jim Wise were vectored towards a MiG-17 while on a BARCAP. Although, as MiG-19 killer Bart Bartholomay recalled, "it took three or four passes for the controller to get him hooked up on the MiG", Kovaleski fired two AIM-9s and Luu Kim Ngo's MiG-17 exploded and crashed into the sea. Ironically, Kovaleski became *Midway's* last combat loss two days later when he and Ens D. H. Plautz were shot down by AAA on a reconnaissance escort mission – both men were rescued.

OVERLEAF
On May 18, 1972, an epic duel was fought above the VPAF's key fighter base at Kep between two MiG-19Ss of the 925th FR and a pair of F-4Bs from VF-161. The "Farmers" would duly suffer their only losses to US Navy Phantom IIs that afternoon whilst attempting to oppose a strike by CVW-15. Here, *Topgun* graduate Lt Henry "Bart" Bartholomay and his RIO Lt Oran Brown, in "Rock River 110", watch their opponent's jet strike the ground at high speed after being struck by an AIM-9 at minimum range. The VPAF pilot had ejected just seconds earlier. (Artwork by Gareth Hector from an F-4 model by Thierry Nyssen and a MiG-19 model by Milviz Inc.)

STATISTICS AND ANALYSIS

During Operation *Linebacker I*, US Navy fighters shot down at least 24 MiGs in 26 aerial combat engagements during the course of 84 combat cruises for the loss of only three US Navy and one US Marine Corps F-4s to VPAF fighters. Seventeen of the communist losses were MiG-17s and MiG-19s, but three of the four F-4 casualties fell to MiG-21s. On May 10, 1972, US Navy Phantom IIs destroyed seven MiG-17s and a MiG-21 without loss, despite having to fight a numerically superior enemy force – this return was a single-day record for the US Navy during the conflict.

The kill-to-loss ratio achieved by Naval Aviators in *Linebacker I* rivalled the best that the US Navy had ever achieved in Vietnam, and it contrasted sharply with that attained by USAF Phantom II units during the same period. Using more inflexible air combat tactics, USAF crews shot down 49 MiGs, but lost no fewer than 25 F-4s in the process. A tactics conference at Udorn Royal Thai Air Force Base in August 1972 enabled three US Navy F-8 pilots to demonstrate the superiority of their "loose deuce" pairs formation in several practice engagements in which they consistently defeated the USAF 432nd

Tactical Reconnaissance Wing's F-4D "welded wing" four-ship formations. The results achieved during these mock dogfights helped to illustrate why, in the previous seven months, the USAF had shot down 25 MiGs at a cost of 20 Phantom IIs while the US Navy's score for the same period had been 25-to-2 in their favour.

During the 43 months of Operation *Rolling Thunder*, US Navy F-4 fighter units sustained only a handful of losses to VPAF MiG-17s and MiG-21s (plus one attributed to a Chinese air force MiG-17), while in return claiming 15 aerial victories – nine of them over MiG-17s – with seven more remaining unconfirmed or "probable" kills. Despite US fighter units enjoying considerable success against the VPAF in 1967, the MiG pilots' share of overall American aircraft losses rose from three per cent in 1966 to 22 per cent in early 1968. The subsequent "bombing halt" enabled the VPAF to expand their numbers still further, and thus offer a much greater threat in the 1971–72 period.

The improvement in the US Navy's fortunes in 1972 can be attributed mainly to the emphasis it placed on training fighter crews in air combat following the introduction of the *Topgun* programme. Naval Aviators learned to use their aircraft more aggressively as true air-to-air fighters, attaining a greater confidence in the Phantom II's capabilities. They were also thoroughly briefed on the strengths and weaknesses of their opponents' aircraft. Indeed, many had faced real MiG-17s and MiG-21s during training, and had lost their first engagements with them in a safe training environment rather than over North Vietnam.

More established F-4 pilots brought up in the "interceptor" philosophy learned to push their Phantom IIs to the limits of their manoeuvrability in dogfights. Squadron schedulers also learnt to put crews with *Topgun* experience in the cockpits when MiGs were expected to show, and 60 per cent of the kills achieved after 1970 were credited to NFWS graduates. Only one *Topgun* crew was shot down by a MiG-17 – VF-103's Lt Bob Randall and Lt "Bat" Masterson on July 10, 1972, their F-4J ("Club Leaf 211") having lost both its radar and radio during a swirling dogfight over Kep.

There was also a change in the way US Navy F-4 crews used their missiles after *Rolling Thunder*. Although the AIM-7 was credited with seven of the fifteen kills up to 1968, its overall reliability was poor. Indeed, its role as the Phantom II's main armament was overtaken by the AIM-9 in the 1971–73 period, when all but two of the 26 kills claimed by Naval Aviators were scored with Sidewinders. However, both missiles demonstrated lamentable performance figures at times.

The majority of MiG-killer crews downed one enemy aircraft, reflecting in part the infrequency of MiG encounters. For long periods North Vietnam's defences were left to AAA and SAMs, and "MiG days" were quite rare for many Phantom II crews. VF-96 had a number of MiGCAP assignments that were certainly on "MiG days". The F-4J NATOPS instructions for pilots stated that, "Proper positioning on the catapult is easily accomplished if the entry is made with enough power to maintain forward motion and the plane director's instructions are followed explicitly". Clearly, the pilot of "Showtime 107" also needed a little manpower to engage with *America's* catapult shuttle in October 1970. (US Navy via Cdr James Carlton)

From August 1 to December 31, 1967, 23 AIM-9B/Ds and seven AIM-7Es were fired by US Navy aircraft, but only five kills were scored. This was a principal factor in the decline of the Phantom II squadrons' kill-to-loss ratio from 4-to-1 in early 1967 to a fraction over 1-to-1 in their favour by the end of the year. In the ten months up to October 1968, some 27 AIM-7s and AIM-9s were launched for only two MiG kills. In the final aerial skirmish of 1968, a pair of VF-143 F-4Bs fired seven AIM-9D and three AIM-7E missiles at two MiG-21s, and all of them failed to guide or detonate correctly. Fortunately, two "Atolls" launched at them in return also missed.

Three F-4 losses were due to hits by "friendly" missiles or damage from missiles that had disintegrated soon after launch. Although both the Ault Report and *Topgun* produced some excellent remedial measures for the maintenance, manufacture and use of the AIM-7, it was seldom used successfully by US Navy pilots for the rest of the war.

Although the US Navy produced just one ace F-4 crew (Lt Randy Cunningham and Lt(jg) Willie Driscoll) during the war, six Phantom II squadrons could claim that honour with five or more confirmed MiG kills – VF-51 (six, including two in F-8 Crusaders), VF-96 (ten), VF-142 (five) and VF-161 (six). To some extent, success depended on the number of combat cruises undertaken and the state of the war over the North at the time. Top scorers VF-96 made a record eight Westpac cruises, of which only two coincided with low levels of bombing activity. Other squadrons such as VF-33 and VF-103 visited *Yankee Station* just once, downing a single MiG each.

For VPAF pilots, there was no set "tour of duty". However, many of the more successful aviators flew combat missions for only three or four years before being

MiG-17 Aces of the VPAF

Name	Kill Claims	Regiment	Service Dates
Nguyen Van Bay	7 (one F-4B)	923rd FR	1964–72
Luu Huy Chao	6	923rd FR	1966–68
Le Hai	6 (one F-4B)	923rd FR	1967–72

Leading US Navy F-4 Phantom II Pilot/RIO "MiG Killers"

Lt Randy Cunningham Lt(jg) Willie Driscoll	1 MiG-21 4 MiG-17s	VF-96	F-4J (AIM-9G)
Lt Matt Connelly Lt Tom Blonski	2 MiG-17s	VF-96	F-4J (AIM-9G)
Lt David Batson Lt Cdr Rob Doremus	2 MiG-17s	VF-21	F-4B (AIM-7E)
Lt Cdr Ron McKeown Lt Jack Ensch	2 MiG-17s	VF-161	F-4B (AIM-9G)

promoted to training or administrative roles. Nguyen Van Bay's seven kills were all logged between June 1966 and April 1967, but he remained in the VPAF until 1972. Of the three pilots credited with six kills, two, Luy Huy Chao and Nguyen Nhat Chieu (two in MiG-21s), fought for only two years.

Although they did not keep personal logbooks, unlike US airmen, many VPAF pilots accumulated huge mission totals. MiG-17F pilot Pham Ngoc Lan's total was 700+ missions and Nguyen Nhat Chieu flew more than 600 (in both MiG-17s and MiG-21s). A number of Phantom II crews flew both *Rolling Thunder* and *Linebacker* missions, but no Naval Aviator claimed MiGs in both operations. The five Cunningham and Driscoll kills came in less than five months in 1972. Squadronmate Lt Steve Shoemaker was on his third cruise when he scored his MiG-17 victory on May 10, 1972, having flown with VF-92 from *Enterprise* in 1966–68.

From 1967 through to war's end, Naval Aviators were usually limited to two combat cruises within 14 months, regardless of the number of missions flown (usually at least 125), while USAF F-4 pilots went home after 100 missions.

Comparing VPAF and US Navy kill claims inevitably raises numerous discrepancies. Both sides vowed that rigid criteria were used to determine the veracity of victory claims. VPAF evidence required gun camera film from MiG-17s and MiG-19s, plus corroboration from witnesses and wreckage on the ground, while the US Navy demanded independent confirmation from witnesses or other intelligence sources.

Naval Aviators flew almost half of their engagements against MiG-17s and MiG-19s, whereas USAF crews faced MiG-21s for nearly 70 per cent of their combats. Some 47 MiG-17s and MiG-19s were claimed to have been shot down (including "probable", "possible" and "unconfirmed" kills) by US Navy units, and 40 received official confirmation – 24 went to F-4 crews.

Ascertaining accurate figures for the VPAF is complicated by several factors. When more than one pilot took part in a kill they all received credit for it. Also, of the 39 F-4 claims, only six were specifically against US Navy Phantom IIs rather than generic "F-4s". Of those, three were attributed by American assessors to AAA or SA-2 SAMs, leaving only the three aircraft piloted by Lt Cdr Clower, Lt(jg) James Teague and Lt Robert Randall as US Navy-confirmed losses to MiG-17s.

Comparison of fighter numbers on opposing sides is hampered by the lack of unclassified figures from Hanoi. After the initial delivery of 35–40 MiG-17s in 1964, supplies of Russian MiG-17Fs and Chinese J-5s were maintained and the force was kept at around 70 for the rest of the war. In 1968–69 they were supplemented by 54 Shenyang J-6s, but by then the MiG-21 was the predominant fighter in the VPAF.

In operational terms, US Navy MiGCAPs of four to eight F-4s normally accompanied strikes, and the VPAF usually responded with about the same number of MiG-17s, often supplemented with a pair of MiG-21s. Although the Task Force on *Yankee Station* could carry up to 72 F-4s spread across three carriers (more during *Linebacker*), operational requirements usually resulted in only one air wing's fighters being available to cover a strike. This in turn meant that MiG and F-4 numbers were often on a par in combat. On occasion, the Phantom IIs found themselves outnumbered when the VPAF put on a maximum defensive effort.

AFTERMATH

The outstanding results obtained by the US Navy's F-4 squadrons in the latter stages of the war were substantially due to the individuals at VX-4, *Topgun* and VF-121, who showed how the Phantom II could be used as a fighter. Despite its disadvantages in size, weight and manoeuvrability when compared with the more nimble MiG-17, the F-4 comprehensively defeated the "Fresco" in a series of battles in 1972.

Tactics such as "lag pursuit" (aggressively manoeuvring the F-4 outside the MiG's turning circle and using its superior speed and roll capability to achieve a firing solution) and negative g manoeuvres gave pilots a real advantage. Shortly after the war, the USAF, whose air combat results had not matched the US Navy's, belatedly introduced realistic ACM training for its F-4 crews, culminating in extensive *Red Flag* exercises staged at Nellis Air Force Base.

Many early F-4Bs, including this 1963-vintage VF-111 sample, were refurbished as F-4Ns with improved ECM equipment and re-lifed airframes. BuNo 151008 soldiered on until a November 1978 flying accident (whilst serving with VF-171) ended its career. (US Navy)

By the time the conflict in Vietnam finally came to end in 1975, the US Navy was already beginning to deploy the Phantom II's successor, the Grumman F-14A Tomcat. It had been conceived in 1969 when the F-4's MiG-killing record was a less impressive one-to-one in combat with MiG-21s. By the mid-1970s the Phantom II was already approaching obsolescence after 15 years of fleet service. The first two Tomcat units flew CAP missions for the evacuation of Saigon in April 1975. The F-14A combined longer-ranging Phoenix missiles and a far more sophisticated fire-control radar for fleet defence within a larger airframe, but one which was more manoeuvrable than the F-4 due largely to its variable sweep wing. It preserved the proven two-seat crew arrangement, and added an integral 20mm cannon to its arsenal.

MiG-21s took over the bulk of the VPAF's fighter duties towards the end of the war, and they remain in service in 2009. The type's performance advantage over the earlier MiGs, and many F-4s, was highlighted by Capt John Nash, who flew both MiG-21s and Phantom IIs. "On my first MiG-21 flight I was chased by a USAF RF-4C. We levelled off at 40,000ft and both lit the burners and unloaded. By the time I hit Mach 2 the RF-4C was five miles behind me at Mach 1.45". This line-up of 921st FR MiG-21MFs also includes a MiG-21UM trainer. (via Peter Mersky)

Despite the arrival of the Tomcat, surviving Phantom IIs continued to serve in the frontline for some years to come until VF-161 made the last F-4 carrier launch on March 25, 1986 from *Midway*. That aircraft was an F-4S, one of around 265 that were re-manufactured F-4Js with a slatted wing for better low-speed handling and combat manoeuvring, updated avionics and smokeless J79-GE-10 engines. They were preceded by 228 F-4Ns (refurbished F-4Bs), and both types continued to fly with US Naval Reserve squadrons until the mid-1980s.

In the VPAF, the MiG-17's frontline service was also extended into the 1980s, albeit as a ground-attack type. Fighter duties had passed to the MiG-21 by 1973, and increasing numbers of these supersonic fighters relegated the MiG-17 to the training role.

The success of this small, simple aircraft was certainly in the minds of Western designers as they pursued different aims from those who produced the large, costly F-14 and F-15 fighters. Lightweight, agile designs that led to the Northrop F-20A, General Dynamics F-16 and, eventually, the McDonnell-Douglas F/A-18 all benefited from the experiences of those who fought MiGs over North Vietnam.

All of these aircraft were originally conceived as dogfighters, and they added better cockpit visibility, fly-by-wire controls (overcoming the F-4's tendency to depart from controlled flight in high angle-of-attack manoeuvres) and cockpits that minimised the pilot's work-load, while letting him keep his eyes on the sky instead of hunting for switches and dials. Thanks to the development of more powerful turbofan engines, all of them boasted a power-to-weight ratio that made the MiG-17 seem sluggish.

The "Fresco's" ease of maintenance was also an influence on later fighters. Groundcrew who had been used to delving in the dark, inaccessible innards of an F-4 to fix elusive faults could now merely pull out a self-tested faulty module and replace it.

The MiG-19's VPAF combat career was over by the autumn of 1972, but a delivery of 24 jets in 1974 enabled a new composite Air Division, the 370th, to be formed the following year. This organisation included the 925th FR, which continued to serve as a training unit until 1980.

FURTHER READING

BOOKS

Belyakov, R. A. and Marmain, J., *MiG – 50 Years of Secret Aircraft Design* (Naval Institute Press, 1994)

Bugos, G. E., *Engineering the F-4 Phantom II* (Naval Institute Press, 1996)

Butowski, P. and Miller, J., *OKB MiG* (Specialty Press, 1991)

Clodfelter, M., *The Limits of Air Power* (The Free Press 1989)

Cunningham, R. and Ethel, J., *Fox Two* (Champlin Fighter Museum, 1984)

Davies, P. E., *Gray Ghosts, US Navy and Marine Corps F-4 Phantom IIs* (Schiffer, 2000)

Drendel, L., *…And Kill MiGs (3rd edition)* (Squadron/Signal 1997)

Drendel, L., *US Navy Phantom IIs in Combat* (Squadron/Signal 1988)

Elward, B. and Davies P. E., *Osprey Combat Aircraft 26 – US Navy F-4 Phantom II MiG Killers 1965–70* (Osprey 2001)

Elward, B. and Davies P. E., *Osprey Combat Aircraft 30 – US Navy F-4 Phantom II MiG Killers 1972–73* (Osprey 2002)

Ethell, J. and Price, A., *One Day in a Long War* (Greenhill Books, 1989)

Francillon, R. J., *Tonkin Gulf Yacht Club* (Conway, 1988)

Friedman, N., *Carrier Air Power* (Conway Maritime Press, 1981)

Gordon, Y., *Mikoyan-Gurevich MiG-17* (Aerofax, 2002)

Gordon, Y., *Mikoyan-Gurevich MiG-19* (Aerofax, 2003)

Gordon, Y. and Dexter, K., *Mikoyan MiG-21* (Midland Publishing, 2008)

Grant, Z., *Over the Beach – The Air War in Vietnam* (W. W. Norton, 1986)

Gunston, B., *Fighters of the Fifties* (Patrick Stephens Ltd, 1981)

Hobson, C., *Vietnam Air Losses* (Midland Publishing, 2001)

Lake, J. (Ed.), *McDonnell F-4 Phantom II, Spirit in the Skies* (Aerospace 1992)

Lawson, R. L (Ed.), *The History of US Naval Air Power* (Temple Press, 1985)

Levinson, J. L., *Alpha Strike Vietnam* (Presidio, 1989)

Long, A., *Tail-End Charlie* (1st Books Library, 2000)

Martin, P., *Hook Code* (Martin, 1991)

McNamara, R. S., *In Retrospect* (Times Books, 1995)

Mersky, P., *Osprey Combat Aircraft 7 – F-8 Crusader Units of the Vietnam War* (Osprey, 1998)

Mersky, P. B., and Polmar, N., *The Naval Air War in Vietnam* (Nautical and Aviation Publishing, 1981)

Michel, M. L., *Clashes* (Naval Institute Press 1997)

Nichols, J. B., and Tillman, B., *On Yankee Station* (Naval Institute Press, 1987)

O'Connor, M., *MiG Killers of Yankee Station* (New Past Press Inc., 2003)

Osinski A., *MiG-17F/Lim-5* (Topshots, Lublin 2005)

Peake, W. R., *F-4 Phantom II, Production and Operational Data* (Midland Publishing, 2004)

Stapfer, H-H., *MiG-17 Fresco* (Squadron/Signal, 2007)

Stapfer, H-H., *MiG-19 Farmer in Action* (Squadron/Signal 1994)

Terzibaschitsch, S., *Aircraft Carriers of the US Navy* (Conway Maritime Press, 1980)

Thomason, T. H., *US Naval Air Superiority* (Specialty Press, 2007)

Thornborough, A. M. and Davies, P. E., *The Phantom II Story* (Arms and Armour, 1994)

Toperczer, I., *Air War Over North Vietnam* (Squadron/Signal, 1998)

Toperczer, I., *Osprey Combat Aircraft 25 – MiG-17 and MiG-19 Units of the Vietnam War* (Osprey, 2001)

Toperczer, I., *Osprey Combat Aircraft 29 – MiG-21 Units of the Vietnam War* (Osprey, 2002)

Wilcox, R. K., *Scream of Eagles* (John Wiley and Son, 1990)

DOCUMENTARY SOURCES

NATOPS Flight Manual NAVAIR 01-245FDB-1 F-4B Aircraft

NATOPS Flight Manual NAVAIR 01-245FDD-1 F-4J Aircraft

NAVAIR 01-45HHA-1T F-8 Tactical Manual (U) 1969

Mikoyan-Gurevich MiG-17 Pilot's Manual

Mikoyan-Gurevich MiG-19 Pilot's Manual

PERIODICALS

Buza, Z., *MiG-17 Over Vietnam*, (Wings of Fame, Volume 8)

Buza, Z and Toperczer, I., *MiG-19 in the Vietnam War* (Wings of Fame, Volume 11)

INDEX